CROSS

AN ANTHOLOGY OF RESILIENCE + HOPE
BY YOUNG SOMALI WRITERS

ROADS

Edited by Marian A. Hassan

ISBN 13: 978-1-63489-287-2

Library of Congress Catalog Number: 2019914516
Printed in the United States of America
First Printing: 2019

23   22   21   20   19   5   4   3   2   1

Minnesota
Humanities
Center

www.mnhum.org

 CLEAN
WATER
LAND &
LEGACY
AMENDMENT
 NATIONAL ENDOWMENT FOR THE
Humanities

This work is funded with money from the Arts and Cultural Heritage Fund that was created with the vote of the people of Minnesota on November 4, 2008.

Cover and interior photos by Chris McDuffie
www.chrismcduffie.photography

Wise Ink Creative Publishing
807 Broadway St. NE, Suite 46
Minneapolis, MN 55413
wiseink.com

To order, visit itascabooks.com or call 1-800-901-3480. Reseller discounts available.

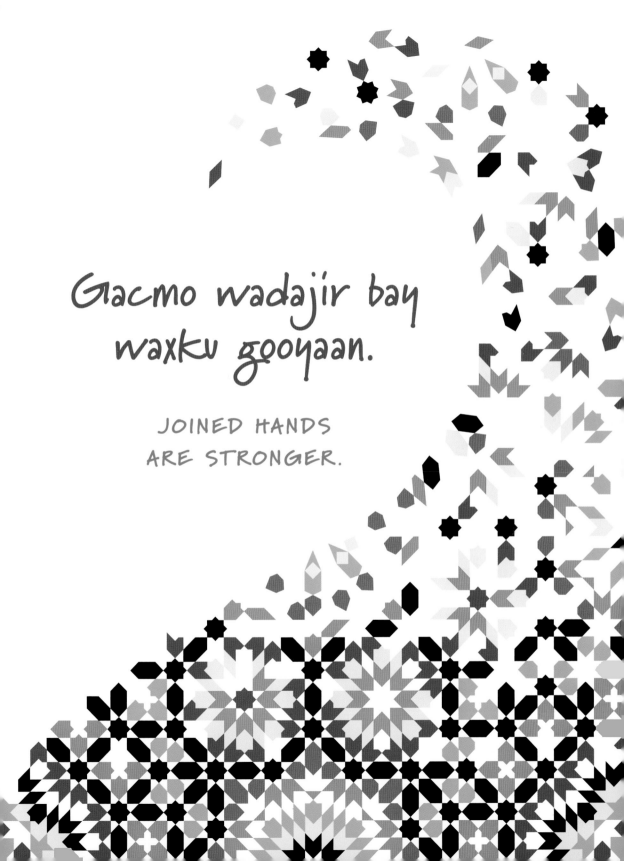

Gacmo wadajir bay
waxku gooyaan.

JOINED HANDS
ARE STRONGER.

Table of Contents

Tiisaba daryeelaa tu
kale ku dara.

THOSE WHO HELP THEMSELVES
CAN HELP OTHERS.

INTRODUCTION

When I was coming of age in a land full of promise, one vastly different from the safe haven of my childhood before the ravages of war, books became my guide. They offered me a sacred space of my own, like the shelter of the stories in my childhood. The library held magic for me, as it would throughout my life, a space of healing and tranquility. I knew stories were healing remedies for all seasons of life. Perhaps they are also the most portable legacies of any culture.

This is an anthology of "absent narratives." These are words that have not previously been committed to writing—happy words, sad words, words about places worlds apart, words of love and longing and long-awaited reunions, and most importantly, words of enduring faith and resilience. *Crossroads* holds a necessary documentation of the words of young people in search of their birthright for peace and belonging while confronting the complex legacies of history, religion, culture, war, and peace. Sharing these stories was necessary for the well-being of the young people crafting the words; we hope it will be equally powerful for those who will read them.

This first-of-its-kind anthology of writings by Somali youth serves as a necessary act of self-representation in this politically challenging time in history, when the authors' multiple identities are so often vilified. There is no other group like the Somali youth, who are at the crossroads of journeys and movements, between cultures, and from a religious tradition often misunderstood and misrepresented. Many of the writers articulate experiences of alienation in a society flawed with ethnic-racial discrimination.

For Somali youth, great empowerment lies in sharing their timely stories of belonging to a resilient community in transition. Equally important, their act of telling will inspire pride in exploring and illuminating the determination of a people invested in rebuilding their lives and moving forward from the impact of war and subsequent displacement.

I believe this human story will also resonate with readers of all ages outside the Somali experience as part of a larger American immigration story. Somalis are like so many others who have embarked on that same journey in search of safety and the American dream. Is that dream still attainable? This anthology sustains the possibility that the American dream remains achievable for the newest immigrants and refugees like the Somalis.

While the Somali community is still recovering from the many wounds of a civil war that has lasted for over twenty-five years, it is important to remember that culture is fluid and never stagnant. Hence, this anthology gives representation to the different experiences in the acculturation process based on levels of education and economic background, age, fluency in the English language, and integration within American society at large. It is particularly important for Somali youth to explore what it means to be American, Muslim, Somali, immigrants, and refugees. The collection explores questions such as: How much of our broader identity defines who we are or want to become? How can a young person negotiate between the values of the old and new cultures, between tradition and transition, and between the weight of their families' hopes and expectations and their own dreams?

THE RICH SOMALI ORAL HERITAGE

This anthology offers an opportunity for Somali youth to reconnect with the enduring wisdom of the Somali oral heritage, which values holding community conversations and story sharing as a healing and life-sustaining practice. While story sharing has always been central to the Somali social discourse, it is now a diminishing practice in the shadows of displacement for first-generation Somali American youth. This anthology helps restore the tradition of sharing first-person stories and experiences. In many ways, this anthology is a documentation of life experiences. Some of the authors chose to share stories they have heard from family members, some even conducting interviews with them. These narratives may serve as a parting legacy for older Somalis to communicate their hopes and dreams to youth. Guidelines were given to the authors about ways to manage interviews (possibly through the creation of story circles) conducted with Somali elders, specifically examining their experiences and the lessons they hope to pass on to a younger generation of Somalis who were born in America or came with their families at a young age and are now living between cultures. They asked questions such as, What is the gift of memory and history? What stories do they want the youth to know and hold onto?

Most importantly, however, it is the youth who construct and share those stories on the page, filtered through their own experiences, hopes, and dreams for the future in a variety of creative formats, forming a tapestry of experiences.

SOMALIS IN MINNESOTA

Minnesota is home to the largest Somali community in the United States. South Minneapolis in particular is a transformed neighborhood, buzzing with Somali-owned restaurants and cafes that are meeting places for local influential people, community centers, weekend cultural and language schools for children, and the ever-popular and much-loved colorful shops in the Somali suuq or bazaars, where you can enjoy delicious shaah (chai) made with sweetened steamed milk with cinnamon, cardamom, and cloves. These are all thriving Somali-owned businesses. Minnesota is changing because of its growing cultural diversity.

On the streets of Minneapolis, St. Paul, and even the suburbs and greater Minnesota, one will often spot traditionally dressed Somali women. Somali women carry on life between cultures, adapting to changing roles in their new lives in America. Their colorful hijabs are now familiar to many Minnesotans. The colors and shades of Minnesota are changing. The sights and sounds and streets are changing. In open markets, even the smells have changed. This anthology will open doors for cross-cultural understanding of the changing face of Minnesota as something good and flavorful, a benefit to our larger society.

MEETING A CRITICAL NEED IN SCHOOLS

One of the places where the changing face of Minnesota is most obvious is our schools. Educators are eager to find new ways to meet the needs of the growing cultural and linguistic diversity in Minnesota. This collection will allow educators to share Somali voices in the readings and discussions taking place in their classrooms.

Stories are also powerful teaching tools for educators. The stories in this anthology will help educators who work with Somali students and families better understand their students who come from a "third culture"—not just home (Somali) culture and not just host (American) culture, but somewhere in between. This collection will not only help educators better understand and connect with their Somali students but also help them find ways to help their non-Somali students better appreciate the experiences of their Somali class-mates.

This anthology will help educators address concepts including what it means to be American; what it means to be born in America while negotiating the charged identities of being a Muslim and a third-culture person whose fluent language may or may not be that of one's parents; and how to succeed in America while coping with loss, missing family members, and displacement. It will also help educators and students explore the options for carrying the dreams of a whole family and community and the complex American history of race, class, and gender inequality.

Educators urgently need resources that specifically highlight the cultural needs of refugee and immigrant youth, in the US but also globally. The narratives of Somali youth in this country will be integral to helping Somali youth make sense of the present as well as the past. This understanding is an essential part of a positive sense of self and identity. This is also necessary to realize the advantages of bilingualism and biculturalism.

CORE CONTENT

The primary voices included in this anthology are those of Somali youth, who themselves wrote stories, presented materials, and collected stories and memories through family con-versations. This collection also incorporates well-chosen samples of proverbs as an offer-ing of inspiration from a nation of poets.

These are the words of young people in transition: growing from childhood into adulthood, balancing very different cultural demands, and navigating their own expecta-tions as well as the expectations of others. They are sharing their stories as a platform upon which to build their own dreams and the dreams of a people who were forced by war to leave one life behind to create another. We hope your life is as changed by reading their words as theirs were through the act of sharing them.

—**Marian A. Hassan**

Samataliye sedkii waa janno.

A GOOD-DOER PROSPERS.

PART I

THE MEMORIES WE CARRY

ARDO MOHAMUD

A Tale of My Own

"We're leaving," Hooyo said as she shed tears of happiness as well as sadness. Even though I was young, I understood what she meant. I questioned myself and our journey from the only home I'd ever known, never to look back again. But I knew I was going to a better place, a place in which I could fulfill my dreams—or, at least, that's what I wanted to believe. Seven years have passed, and a lot has changed. My feet no longer touch the beautiful, warm soil of Ethiopia but rather the cold, white snow of Minnesota.

My family and I moved to Minnesota during the winter. The snow blinded our eyes and the wind blew everything away. My siblings and I weren't able to attend school for months while our paperwork was being processed. In the meantime, I stayed as a guest in a relative's house. Later on, we moved to a shelter house in North Minneapolis, started attending Anne Sullivan School, and then transferred to Jefferson Community School. The spring blossoms started to bloom, but my experience in Minnesota was still dark. I knew my "hellos" and "how are yous," but the language barrier was difficult for me. I sat in class with strangers, not knowing the language they spoke, without a clue as to what was going on. After a while, I got my grip and became fluent in English in under a year. Although the language barrier was out of my way, there was more to unfold.

A year turned into two years, two turned into three, and so on. I talked on the phone with my stepsister, aunts, cousins, and other family living in Ethiopia, including my grandmother, whom I had never spoken with before. Over the summer, I talked on the phone with my grandmother for the first time in my life. I burst into deep tears when she asked our whereabouts. Then a sudden thought came upon me: How did my own mother cope with the feeling of not seeing her mother for over twenty years?

One of the saddest days of my life took place last week. I had just gotten back from school and was headed to a corner store to buy food with my mom. "I want to go back home," she said, tearing up. I was surprised and scared at the same time because my mom is brave and can keep herself calm even in the hardest times. I asked why she was crying, and I was silenced by what I heard. March 19, 2018, marked the death of my maternal aunt. My life suddenly turned dark, and all I could do was cry myself to sleep. Knowing a loved one is dead and being unable to be there is one of my greatest fears. Coping with the thought of missing family members is the hardest thing my family and I are going through at the moment.

Recently, I was asked what it means to be in between cultures and what I remember from back home. Living in between two different cultures can cause you to lose your sense of identity. I don't have trouble with my identity as a Somali Muslim woman because I left Ethiopia as a grown-up nine-year-old with a strong foundation of identity. I use English for a good part of the day, but I make sure I speak Somali just as often to keep my home tongue with me for the rest of my life. As we say in Somali, "Afka hooyadaa waa dahab." Therefore, I know how to keep a balance between the two cultures.

I asked my parents about how they made it to Ethiopia. Both my hooyo and my aabo escaped the Somali civil war in 1990 and got separated from their parents and siblings at the age of fifteen. They spent a decade or two in Ethiopia before moving to the United States.

As we all know, the West is not favorable toward Muslims, so as a Muslim Somali woman, I have to look out for myself more often. A lot went on during the first few months of 2018. On April 3, "Punish a Muslim Day" was introduced around the world. Throwing acid at a Muslim woman's face supposedly gives you points. A few days ago, an innocent Muslim man walking on the streets of the UK was stabbed to death. These incidents cause a deep fear in my heart. I fear for my own family and friends as well as for myself. Living in a country where you're not welcome is never easy; you never know what tragedy is yet to happen. Throughout the years I lived in Minneapolis, I haven't had a personal encounter with anyone who would have something against me because I'm a Muslim, but I'm aware of how other Muslim people are treated due to how the media portrays Islam. Otherwise, I've had an amazing experience living in Minnesota. I am able to attend Southwest High School as a sophomore going into junior year. I dream of staying in school no matter what happens, and here I am, getting a step closer to my dreams every day.

SAFI MOHAMED

The Dreams I Carry

From childhood, I heard stories
The same words over and over
The story of my country,
My parents' need to find closure
Open wounds, battlefields covered in blood
Gushing from our soldiers, turning into a flood
Families flee, wanting a better life
Only to find out America was just a hype
I carry my family's dreams as though they were mine
Become a doctor, go back to Somalia, you can actually save lives
The pressure of becoming this great person is building up
Who I wanna be and what I'm expected of
I'm trying, but is it really enough?
Expectations I'm trying to live up to
The dreams I carry

SARA OSMAN

executive order 13769.

i.
tonight,
i am far from home
wandering aimlessly from shop to shop
until i lock eyes with a woman standing by the pillar

we assess each other openly
the high cheekbones
and wide forehead

i know my people.

she leads me to the back and shows me off to her coworkers
they kiss my cheeks and i relish in the warmth

she pours me a cup of tea
and explains how her family fled Somalia,
only to now flee Syria

chaos follows us, she sighs.
i nod—this i know well.

i want to leave here, nothing grows in the desert, she says
our papers went through and we are headed to Minnesota next year, inshaa Allah
there, we will start over, again.

i wonder if she saw through me
i'm sorry eedo,

i didn't mean to slip

we sit in silence for a little while longer
as we part,
            she embraces me tightly
                    ajanabiga iska ilaali, she whispers to me

i leave
but dammit,

i should've said something back.

ii.

as a child, my mother and i would take long walks
her niqaab tightly secured on her face
sitting still made her restless, she claimed
now i wonder if she was trying to keep from running

we had rituals
she and i
Qur'an in the morning
and du'as at sunset

the lessons i learned early:
insert steel into your spine so you never bend
do not bow your head
this shame is not yours, release it

let your hijab ripple on the breeze
let them stare

dodge their swings and wipe their spit from your face
remember to *always* spit back

yes, to be Muslim is to submit
but never to this

Bixiiyaa waa Eebbe.

GOD IS THE GIVER.

FIRDOWSA HASHIM

Identity

Identity. It is something that every one of us in this world struggles with. We think we know who we are, but then a new part of ourselves surfaces. Whether it is religion, culture, or ideology, we wonder, "What do I identify with?" My parents are from a faraway land, the country where they were born was ravaged by war, and we are here so far away. I feel as if I have two different identities. I live in two different worlds, constantly trying to satisfy both. I am influenced by the American culture yet surrounded by the culture of my ethnicity. It's difficult to find a balance, to acculturate but not assimilate, to keep from losing a part of myself in order to make room for the other.

When I'm at home and with my family, I act differently than when I am in public or at school. It isn't a drastic change in behavior, but little nuances that I add or take away in certain circumstances. Because I am deeply engaged in the American culture, I sometimes feel that my ethnic culture is slipping away and my mother tongue is disappearing. I try my hardest to always stay with my family's traditions. Every day, I work to reinforce the mother tongue that is embedded within my identity.

Being born in America has given me countless opportunities. Not all opportunities are equal, but I am thankful for the access to opportunities that I wouldn't have anywhere else. I feel that, being born in America, I am held to a certain standard. I have heard this from my relatives back in Somalia. I am expected to succeed in everything I do, and there is this weight on my shoulders that seems never to come off. However, I have amazing friends I can count on and a bright future. Because of all that happened in Somalia, I know I would not have gotten this kind of life and opportunity if my parents had stayed there.

My parents experienced a very difficult and unimaginable time because of the civil war in Somalia. Both my parents had to travel separately from their families for a period. My mother had to find a path for her family to travel while bullets were raining down. My father had to run back home from school to make sure his family was safe while the capitol building was being attacked. Even when they got out of Mogadishu alive, the refugee camps in Kenya weren't any better. My parents, as well as everyone else in that situation, had to overcome starvation, illness, and lack of water. Both my parents came to America by getting help from the United States. Here they were able to make a better life for themselves with more opportunities.

While I have these opportunities, I want to make my family proud and to give them the world. I want to make my parents proud and repay them for all they did for me and my sisters. They sacrificed so much to put my sisters and me through school, to feed us, to put clothes on my back, and to raise us in a new world, where the culture was unfamiliar and the language was extremely hard. In addition to school, I can't forget my obligations as a Muslim. It is important to study my religion and follow its rules. My faith is the most important part of my identity.

When I was younger, I was bullied because of my religion. I was called names, such as "bald-headed," for wearing my hijab. The kids would say, "Is your hair dirty? Is that why you hide your hair?" I cried many times because of those remarks. I knew my hair wasn't dirty or ugly. Somali people are naturally beautiful. I knew I had long, beautiful hair, but those words still hurt so much.

Before living in St. Paul, I lived in Fargo, North Dakota. That was where my parents were placed when they came to America. Though it was a better life for them, they experienced discrimination. At the store where my mother worked, her supervisor told her to take off her hijab because he didn't like it. She refused to take it off and quit her job. My mother told me she didn't work in Fargo again because there weren't many jobs to choose from at the time, and she was also hindered by her qualifications. At the jobs she did qualify for, she wasn't allowed to wear her hijab.

There are many things I fear, like spiders and snakes, but I never thought I would have to fear being a Muslim. What on Earth happened to that "freedom of religion" in the American Constitution? I want to express my faith and who I am without fear. This fear was born and grew in the hearts of some people after the 2016 election. People hate what is different and what they don't understand. Why don't they try to understand? We are human like they are human—maybe they too search for guidance in a higher power just like we do. They probably have a family, just like us, and people they love, just like us. I have heard people saying that all Muslims are terrorists, but that is not true. So many Muslims in this world suffer because others have that mindset. I am no terrorist! I have never hurt anyone, and Islam is against hurting anyone.

I feel bad because Islam has been associated with violence. It weighs down on me knowing the religion and the faith I cherish are viewed in a bad light because of ugly misunderstanding.

Aqoonla'aani waa iftiinla'aan.

WITHOUT KNOWLEDGE IS DARKNESS.

NAWAL ABDI

Memories

I was taken away from my home country as a little girl in 2012. When I'm asked what Kenya was like, it is hard to remember. All I have now are my memories up to age nine.

My first day of school in Kenya was one of the most memorable days of my life. I remember waking up and putting on my blue-and-white plaid uniform. That was the first time I put on my own uniform. Every day, I would wear my aunt's clothing and try reading her books, even though I knew I couldn't read. My aunt was always looking at her book and would read page after page. I looked up to her and hoped, one day, when I went to school, I too would be able to read a book fluently. I remember going to school with my neighbors and how we made jokes about the teachers along the way. I didn't really understand what they were saying because I didn't know the teachers, but I laughed along. One story I found funny was about one particular teacher who would blame the older siblings for the things their young siblings did. One day, my aunt Bisharo was chewing gum and that teacher caught her. He took the gum, went to my other aunt Bushro's class, and stuck the gum on her hijab. After school, I was so happy that I had to tell everyone about what happened.

I remember the day my mom told me we would move to America in a couple years if we were approved or selected. She told me, "We have a chance to start a new life, with better opportunities for you and your sister." That is when heartbreak started. I remember seeing her looking at a board that had names of people moving to the next stage. She would look for her name with an excited expression, and it would disappear when she didn't find it. At night I could hear her crying because she knew she had lost yet another chance for our family to have a new start, a new life for ourselves.

"I spent my childhood in Somalia," she told me. "The days I spent there were the best. I loved the beautiful blue sea. The beach in Somalia was breathtaking. I can't express it enough. It is a story untold and a sight unseen. My favorite part was seeing familiar faces. I always felt at home. In 1991—I remember it like it was yesterday—I was outside on the balcony when I heard the first bomb drop. I thought it was the end of the world. I was terrified before I noticed there were tears rolling down my cheek."

I remember my last time in Kenya. We all got on an airplane for our first time ever. After a while, I went to sleep. My six-year-old sister, on the other hand, didn't sleep. She was too excited. The minute I woke up, she started telling me about the people, and how the flight attendant was cool. I laughed at her in disbelief. There was a group of close friends of my mom who were there for us through hard times. We were separated from them in New York, and that was the last time I saw them. The times when we were with them were the most memorable. Even though they were much older, they still treated me with respect. As time went by, I began to forget their faces. Now I can barely name any of them. At times like that, I feel disappointed in myself. "How could you forget about the people you spent half your childhood with?" I ask myself that question every single day.

Those are the memories I want to cherish every day. Sometimes I wish I had more memories of Kenya. At times, I've asked my mom how much she loved Kenya. She always talks about the beautiful times she had there. Her most beautiful memories are the ones she met with her sibling. She talks about how she would do things that got her in trouble and get punished for it. When my mom tells me these stories, I can see that she really misses Kenya. When we first came to America, we struggled because we were in an unknown place with no help. Unlike Kenya, America is so different from Somalia.

"Three years into the Somali war, we immigrated to Kenya," said my mother. "We stayed with other family members until we got on our feet. We applied to become refugees in 2001. We luckily got accepted and immigrated to America in 2005."

My first day of school in America was the total opposite of my first day of school in Kenya. I was not familiar with my surroundings, and I didn't understand the language. The worst part was that I didn't know anyone there. After a while, I met some kids who had just moved to our apartment building. We helped each other with our homework. At that time, math was easiest for me because I only needed to understand the concept and not the language. I never understood the things they taught in school.

As I cherish my memories from Kenya, my younger brother has none. He came to America when he was only one year old. Once in a while, he asks me to tell him what

Kenya was like. Whenever he asks, I give a pitying face. I tell him about the memories I have from Kenya. He always has the same reaction: amazement. "I wish I were there," he tells me.

"When I arrived in America, it was a great culture shock," my mother told me. "It was the first time I saw so many white people. I didn't know any English. I came here with no educational background. Everything felt new to me, and I didn't know where and how to start my life here. It was really hard for me to get a job here because of my old age and with no education. I got really lucky to get a job. The money was enough to support my family."

No matter the hardships, we were able to overcome and support each other.

MOHAMEDAMIN HUSSEIN

We Know

The world is changing
The time is raging
We are the next generation
Right now, our real nation
Is falling apart
Our story
Our art
As you can see
Our world is getting dirty

We are causing this by losing everything
The poets who used to sing
Are growing old

The entire Muslim threshold
Is about to burst
We aren't unique anymore
This is the worst
We took the culture
Of those we met first
We got conquered
We lost our honor
We aren't the kids of tomorrow
We are the kids of today
That is worst kind of cliché

Am I right?
We aren't part of the light
We are losing hope
We can't reach the rope
To bring us back

Our parents
Are the only ones who hold our culture strong
The kids think they don't belong
And I say
No

I know kids, and it's all for show
We know
We can't reach the rope
To bring us back

Our parents
Are the only ones who hold our culture strong
The kids think they don't belong
And I say
No

I know kids, and it's all for show
We know

SHADIA ESSA

Hooyo Macaan's Home

dagayso, shaakadayda si ficcan udagayso.

I turn around, and they shove me. The pots and pans clash, and curtains end up on the floor.

"Look!"

"Golka ku xiga baadh, wiil bay haystana." *Search in the next room. I know they have a son.* They run into the next room, where awaits Hooyo and seven-year-old Walaal, sitting in the far left corner of a dark room where you need your ears as your eyes and your eyes as your ears.

"Grab them." They grab Hooyo. My brother sees that Hooyo and I dressed my brother Aboowe Ahmed as a gabadh yar named Haawo so they wouldn't take him. "What?! Where is the son? Wiilka aaway." In their rush, they forget to look closely, so they miss what they are searching for and get caught in the moment.

"Sir, let's go!" They leave, and Hooyo Macaan's delicate body hits the hard rock floor. She starts crying tears so sweet as they drip down her precious face and onto Abowo's desiccated lips.

Aboowe rips out of the clothes as if he's an angry libaax. "Why?! Why do you need to put me in clothing that's meant for females? Maxaad iigu gelinaysaa dhar gabadh loogu talo ga?"

"Why?" Hooyo looks at him with her heart-melting eyes, which are so gaali that the second she looks, he sits. "Your father died because of these men!" I have no idea what she is trying to say in Somali.

Remembering

Aabbo died years ago. I remember it was a hot summer day, about 90 degrees. We were inside, in a room where if you sat in comfort no one else would be able to fit inside. He was telling us a story about the beautiful beach waves and the gorgeous farmlands. He said every word as if it were his last. Describing it as if it were his last breath, smiling as if it were the best day of his life. However, in his eyes, if you looked at them at the right time with the right angle, you could tell he was counting every laugh we laughed, every tear we cried, every smile we smiled, and every time we sighed.

This roller coaster–like story Aabbo was telling was a symbol. He knew something we didn't. Aabbo knew danger was coming. Aabbo was a man so mindful, however, with a tongue that spoke words so foreign, a mind that was dangerous, a heart so pure, and a soul so humble and unforgettable.

As he was telling the story, two large shadows came upon us. Then our father was dragged across the door and onto the naxaris laan, sweaty, and deeg-printed streets. BANG! BANG! Allah u naxaristo, that was the last we heard of Aabbo Macaan.

Hooyo says, "For every breath I take, I think of him. And with every breath I take, always know I will be keeping you safe. The very thought of you gone in an instant kills me." The wind blows the door open, and we all look toward it. Hooyo says, "Now, go close the door. Ahmed, you need to put these on." Days go by, and we desperately hold on for dear life. Months go by and fear starts to get in the frame. Years go by, and all connection has been lost. Somalia, my motherland, has been taken by people so cruel that we are suffering in the hands of our own people. My motherland waa lugugu ciyaaray. My home has been ripped apart. However, my home is still a place where when you walk, the warm, sugar-like sand massages your bare feet, where the eedaan is heard right from your own bedroom, where the famous Hooyo Macaan waves are active even on restless nights. My home still has the foundation of a home. However, dadkii, our people, are waiting for other muuminiin to fix our own mistakes. Soomaaliya wali rajo Ayaan ka leeyahay. Soomaaliya ha burburin. Soomaaliya ha la soo nooleeyo!

DAHABO MOHAMED

Pride

"She's a part of that religion that condones violence."
When I walk down the streets of the country I call home, that is all I hear.
Does my existence cause you some sort of harm?
You stare, point, and call me nothing but a terrorist.
You try to shame me because I choose to follow a religion that I know as peace.

I walk down the streets of the country I am a citizen of with pride and dignity.
But why is it that when I walk those streets, I hear nothing but hate?
All you say is, "Don't worry, guys. She will get kicked out soon."
Do you not realize these remarks do not scare me one bit?
But why do you want me gone so bad?
What did I do to you?

Is it my fault you associate me with Bin Laden?
Is it my fault that when you see me, you think ISIS? I give you the benefit of doubt.
I smile when I see you walk down the streets. I don't associate you with Hitler.
I don't think you're a part of the KKK.
But why is it that you can't give me that benefit of doubt that I give you?

All I hear are the lectures of why would I ever want to follow a religion of hate.
But in your eyes, it's no lecture. You just frame it like you want the best for me.
But did it not occur that your opinion is no factor
when I decide the religion I want to practice?
Your curiosity on why I wear a black scarf on a hot summer day
does not make me question the religion that I call peace.

I walk down the streets of the country I was born in with nothing but pride.
But all I hear are my fellow citizens trying to tear me down.
You telling me to go back to my "pretty disgusting" country sounds foolish on your part.
This is my country just as much as it is yours.

So please don't bother me when I walk down the streets
of the country I will soon be able to vote in with nothing but my pride
So please don't give me an unasked-for lecture when I walk down the streets
of the country that is my joy with nothing but my pride.

SARA OSMAN

holy.

your mother leaves the house every morning
and returns in the evening with food for someone,
anyone
but nothing for her
breaking off pieces of herself to keep you fed
when the bread runs dry

you watch someone do a thing enough times
and it becomes scripture

this is how we have always been

girls learn to give, boys learn to take
it is our dhaqan, they say
our way of life
our women should be satisfied with sacrifice
it is holy

being this far from God has allowed them to transgress

you are woman so you are sinful, they say
they do not know how to build
only to destroy
        so, they take their time
                and pull you apart,
slowly and deliberately
they do not notice you have stopped breathing
        long ago

as you wait for death
you whisper to the earth about the crimes they have committed
against you and this body
and she whispers back,
"me too"

nothing is sacred to men.

AYAN HASSAN

Recovering

I used to live with my grandparents in a refugee camp in Ethiopia. When I was six, one of my neighbors invited me to go climb a tree. The tree wasn't that high, but when I got to the top branch, it broke and I fell to the ground. I went home and went to sleep without talking to my grandma. The next morning, I woke up with my arm all bruised up and my family asking me what had happened. I refused to tell them.

After a few weeks of having my arm all bruised up, my grandparents called a cultural doctor to check my arm. The doctor told my grandparents, "Her arm is broken in three different places, and we'll try to fix it." He said he would look at it again within two weeks. My arm got worse, and it reached a level where I couldn't even move it. When we went to the doctor again, he told us, "I can't do anything about it."

My grandparents borrowed some money from the neighbors and took me to the hospital. The doctor told my grandparents the worst news in the world: the only choice was to cut my arm off. My grandpa refused it and said he'd keep me as I was. Two days later, my grandpa saw another cultural doctor. When he touched my arm and tried to check it, my arm popped.

That was the moment I felt I lost everything I had as a child. My arm was infected, and I had a fever. I was turning seven years old, but I wasn't able to go to school. I was illiterate. My grandma made a bed for me and kept me inside the house. One of our neighbors said there was a specialty doctor who came to Ethiopia once a year, so I might have a chance to survive. We went to the hospital, and after the doctor told us that the infection was getting worse, we scheduled a surgery for the next day.

After six hours of surgery, the doctor told my grandparents that he took out all the infection. But that wasn't the end: after four years, the infection came back to my arm.

One night I woke up in pain in the middle of the night and felt a bone coming out of my arm. The bone was getting bigger every day while my arm got worse. The leaders of the refugee camp said they would help us, and they talked to the International Organization for Migration (IOM) about coming to America. When they saw my arm, they told us they would put us on a waiting list.

On March 3, 2013, we came to the United States, the land of freedom and opportunity for us. I had my third surgery on August 7, 2013, at the Hennepin County Medical Center in Minneapolis, Minnesota. Today, my arm is healthy and I can use my other hand.

I am now a student at Wellstone International High School and beginning my senior year. While learning English has not been easy, I have learned that it's important to never give up and continue to learn each and every day. This was the same lesson I used when I was recovering from my arm injury. Since coming to the United States, I have been involved in many activities, such as student council, the Somali Student Association, the Muslim Student Association, the girls' varsity soccer team, and the Power of the Youth program at Pillsbury House. These activities have prepared me for my future by helping me learn English, communicate with others, and work with people who come from different countries and cultures.

ALI ALI

Somalia's Symbol

Roses are red, and while violets are blue,
I find you enchanting when I feel gloom.
There are thousands of stars, but I can only see one,
The star in the Somali flag that's always won.

The blue background blends with the star,
Like no other, it shines by far,
Like a car's headlight that shines so bright,
When a storm's a-coming which will seem fit,
Like in baseball when there's an inning, but nothing went in.
Like Abdul-Jabbar we take shots that go in,
There's nothing like losing
We strive for victory, we can grow wings,
Somalia, the land of the lion.

MOHAMED HASSAN

Our Journey

My name is Mohamed Hassan, and I am turning thirteen this year. I was born April 4, 2005. Something happened three years ago in my home country, South Africa, that now I am going to talk about.

It all started when I was playing in the woods with my brothers. Although my mother did not allow us to play there, we did. Sometimes we got in trouble and sometimes we did not because we washed the dishes and cleaned the mat and the beds. We did this so that my mother would get comfortable and not shout at us when we played in the woods. My mother said the woods were dangerous because there were thieves, killers, and drug dealers out there. I thought my mother was exaggerating, so I kept on playing in the woods, although my brothers stopped. When I came back one day, my cousins who lived next door looked very solemn. I entered the house and everyone inside was crying.

My mother tried to tell me what happened, but she was too sad, so she whispered it into my ear: "An incident happened. Your father got shot, and he is at the hospital right now." I was shocked and I did not close my eyes for about three minutes. Suddenly, I started crying and could not stop. I could not control my tears. It was too much to bear that someone had deprived me of my father, and somehow I thought it was my fault. My brother Abdiaziz was ignorant, and he did not believe it. Then he turned around and tears fell on the ground.

All of us waited for hours for the hospital's response. One by one, we fell asleep, but my mother did not sleep for the whole night. Her eyes were very red. After I woke up, I asked her to sleep while tears fell down my cheeks to my chin. She refused. My oldest brother, Walid, had had trouble sleeping since he was little. They had given him this medicine to make him sleep that came in a peach-colored bottle with a green cap, and luckily he still used it. He took a cup, filled it with water, added the medicine, and gave it to our mother. Soon she was asleep. After three weeks, my brother told us to go back to school and dugsi and to keep our academic grades up.

When we came back from school, we finally got what we were waiting day and night for. The hospital called. They said my dad was going to survive and that he was shot on top of the heart, not the heart itself. He must have felt excruciating pain, but he was going to return after a week. Although the news was bittersweet, I was so glad that tears of joy came flooding like a thunderstorm over the ocean. I was anxious to see my dad. My mother said to be vigilant around our father or we would make the pain worse. After an hour or so, an officer came to our house to talk about the incident with my dad. My mother said it was not a coincidence. The officer said he would make it his obligation to capture the men who shot my father.

After three weeks, my dad came home. I shouldered my emotion and I asked him, "Why can't we just kill the men who shot you?"

My dad said, "When a man is caused suffering, he can sleep. But if he causes suffering, his mind will never rest."

Aqoon xumo abaar
ka daran.

IGNORANCE IS WORSE
THAN DROUGHT.

IFRAH MANSOUR

Somalia Calling

*A poem commemorating the catastrophic October 14, 2017,
bombing in Mogadishu, Somalia.*

Walaaley Macaan [my sweetness]
Did you hear her call for you underneath the rambling earth?
Walaaley Macaan
Did you see her expand her mouth like a child coming out of a mother's heaven?

Walaaley Macaan
Did we witness a single truck bombing
claiming the lives of more than 300, still counting.
Affecting the lives of more than 600, still counting?

Walaaley Macaan
Under a second detonation,
yet over a week of digging,
souls, still hovering over the skies of Mogadishu,
the world, still watching us like a million-dollar action movie
Walaaley Macaan
Did we think about what we'll say
to little brown Mohamed when he asks?
Aabbo, did you stand still?
Hooyo, did your blood not move?
Abaayo, did you see the head of a child no mother present to claim?
Aboowe, did you watch them dig only to find an unrecognizable Somali?
Walaalayaal, is our humanity trapped in the darkening ozone?

Remembering

Walaaley Macaan
did you hear home call for us, underneath the aching earth?

Walaaley Macaan
We might be from a nation seemingly too close to death and destruction,
but death and destruction of this ill caliber have shocked us to our core

Walaaley Macaan
Our lives might be under a constant
fear of injustice, but life has always been
a flickering faynuus

Walaaley Macaan,
tell the newspapers, No,
we don't walk around with our shrines already in our hands
we're stubborn survivors,
we got pens and papers in our hands
and "How can I help you?"
and "How can I uplift you?" in our hearts

Walaaley Macaan
Today we send strings of tears across the globe,
we ache for wounds without a flesh
Today, we buried our kin limb by limb,
bodies without body parts
and babies without faces

Walaaley Macaan
There is nothing more unifying
than the pain of having to bury our children,
our future, before us

Walaaley Macaan
Today, our hands are raised to the heavens,
sending strings of prayers, our bodies are present,
ready to show our kids watching us,
what love looks like in the face of tragedy,
what strength feels like in the midst of catastrophic pain,
and what courage looks like in the midst of fearful times

Walaaley Macaan
Our children are clicks away
from witnessing our idleness or our action
our Somaliness is in your breath, share it with love
our history is in your fingertips, write it with love
our humanity is in your voice, teach it with love

Walaaley Macaan
Home is calling us
and it left us a message of love stronger than hate,
strength stronger than fear

Walaaley Macaan
Somalia is still calling

Cidlo ciirsi ma leh.

HELP CANNOT BE FOUND
WHERE THERE IS NO ONE.

PART II

LIVING BETWEEN CULTURES

SARA OSMAN

maternal moon phases/faces.

part i. first quarter

in another life,
thunderstorms were my call home
my mother gathered us so we could watch the sky unleash her fury
we sat by the screen door,
watching the soothing rhythm of the rain and thunder
until we became mesmerized by the harmonic conflict
we sought to recreate it daily
and failed miserably every time
but that did not hinder our attempts to reach above our stations

my mother kept her eyes to the sky constantly
she particularly loved the moon
if there was a full moon,
she would remind us to pray
if the moon had a reddish tint,
she'd insist that we look out for each other as there would be troubles ahead
isoo dhawaada, she'd say.
and let me tell you of the nights the moon kissed the land in Xamar.
she'd recite how the moon seemed to land on the beach
and how they spent the entire night awake, in prayer, in awe

part ii. full moon
i spent most of my childhood waiting for days to end
and welcomed night like an elder whose visits brought gifts
but are the stars not gifts?
watch how they dance gracefully in the presence of the moon,
their mother,
forever holding her captivated audience
she'd watch their shows with a faint smile,
the way my mother watched us grow.

every genesis begins with pain
but our mother masked ours with teachings in
good intentions and orthodox behavior
her face glowed down on us, illuminating our fears
she would summon us home every night
and would wait until we were promised to see day

only then would she allow herself some rest.

part iii. third quarter
in this life, death comes by sky
drone strikes incite nightmares during daylight
notice how we do not need to sleep to feel terror
only under the blanket of night does peace fall

we learned life lessons this way
gave name to evils without *haqq*
the moon saw all and withheld her verdict
but the wickedness of humanity was too much to handle
and she lost a piece of herself every night, to be eventually born anew

we witnessed atonement through her rebirth
a death she did not deserve but a price she would pay
the same way women reconciled monthly menses as payment for ancestral penance
we take
and we take
and we take
greed no more improper than self-sacrificial tendencies
this is how they will find us when she has no more to give:
hands reaching out, cupped in invocation.

part iv. new moon
nowadays, we don't watch thunderstorms
we live in them
our lives existing in the same melodic and organized chaos as the sky
we move in natural rhythm,
without breaking beat,
in sync
like the rain that used to drop outside our door in a past life,
a long time ago
we live on this earth like lightning;
sharp and quick, never making the same mistake twice
because we, unlike our mother, will not be born again

though all that awaits is judgment
we do not relish in damnation
so, my mother still has her eyes on the moon,
still reminds us to pray
always reminds us to pray
and we,
functioning in strange and recent times with archaic convictions,
keep our hands up,
to the moon,
praying.

the headline read: "trump issues Muslim ban"
it is january

she is the first thing i think of,
my unnamed eedo in Amman

i do not have any way of contacting her
i cannot check to see if she survived
the carnage we elected

i remember her smile
and if i shut my eyes,
i can taste her tea

today, i hate this place.

tomorrow, i will still hate this place.

i think of how i prefer the spit to *this.*
                    whatever *this* is.

Gar iyo geeri loo siman.

DEATH AND JUSTICE
AFFECT ALL MEN
EQUALLY.

WASIMA FARAH

Using my words

My pieces explore the options of carrying the dream of a whole family, of a community, and of oneself. My first piece expresses feeling trapped in someone else's dream and not being true to yourself. This matters to me because I'm at a stage where I'm transitioning from high school to college and being pressured to follow only one dream that my parents are familiar with. My second piece expresses speaking out strongly with whatever opinion or thought I have. This matters to me because that's what I want to achieve—to be unapologetic about my dreams and opinions. This piece is also conveying that my pain and anger are valid. I want the readers to understand how strong one can be when they realize their dreams and don't give up on them.

UGBAD BARUD

Integrity

My desire to make a difference began at seven years old. It was the day my mother gave birth to my baby brother. She had many problems, and she didn't have anyone to help her deliver the baby. My baby brother died after many hours of labor. My mother began bleeding so heavily that she went into a coma for two hours. Many mothers who live in a refugee camp die when they give birth because they don't have a midwife to help them. That day, I decided to become a midwife. I wanted to make sure giving birth did not mean dying. My mother encouraged me and told me I could become a midwife and that I would help mothers and babies be safe during childbirth.

My name is Ugbad Barud. I am from Ethiopia, but my parents are from Somalia. I have three sisters and two brothers. I live with my mother and my father. I have lived almost four years in the United States. When I lived in Ethiopia, I had a hard life because Ethiopia was not my home country and they didn't like Somali people. I lived in a refugee camp with all my family. I had little education because my parents didn't have money for me to go to school. I went to a school for refugees, but that school didn't have much to offer for good education. However, we did not have money to pay for a special school, and when you are poor and living in a refugee camp, you go to the school offered. I wanted to go to a real school in Ethiopia and be a good student, but they told me, "You cannot come here! You're a refugee, and refugee people don't come to this school."

I don't have to live in Ethiopia anymore. My life is better in America. I live with both of my parents now. The first time I came to the United States, I lived in Missouri. I started school there, but it was hard for me. Then my mother and my father said, "Guys, we have to move to Minneapolis because some of our family lives there." When I moved to Minneapolis, I started going to Wellstone International High School. Wellstone is the best school for me. I will never forget my Wellstone teachers because they helped me a lot when I came here. When I first arrived, the students asked me questions I did not understand. But now I have been here for almost four years, and this year is my last at Wellstone. I have become involved in some programs at my school, such as student council, the Muslim Association, the Somali Students Association, the Lions Clubs, and Jobs for America's Graduates (JAG). I work in a lot of volunteer programs, like at the Mall of America, Confederation Community, food drives, the Minneapolis immigrant welcoming event, Furthering Achievement through a Network of Support (FANS), and a program for bikes and recreation.

After high school, I want to go to college and study to become a midwife. I want to help mothers live in this world, especially mothers who live in refugee camps, because I still remember the day when my mother had a baby without a midwife.

MOHAMED ALI

Fallen Soldier

We are family
Fought against inequality
Clearly they were bothered
Because we are colored

We are related
They instigated
We are the same
Disrespected, what a shame
Awoken Soldier

We asked to help us God
We started to nod
At the changes that happened
Thought we lost racism in the past

Came back to haunt us even worse than before
Destroying our ego, cracking our core
Racism is still there, no matter how hard you try
People hating each other, wanting to see me break and cry

Young but free
Not afraid of my race or being a Somali
Both Somali and Muslim
Two words associated with terrorism

Asking myself just why
Treat me different
Many thoughts flowing my brain
Yet I understand that greatness is my aim

Beautiful men and women
For every person a story
I am like you and you are like me
A story of escaping a war-torn country
Many young kids, searching for food, while crying out hungry

Witnessing the tears of a child
Yet we are looked at as if we are maniacs while others' behavior is mild
At times life does get wild

Now they want to build a wall
That's very tall
Separate us 'cause of where we came from
Want to wash us out as if we were germs

Humans, different colors, everyone on a different page
The system is broken, trying to place us in a cage

I'm black, and that isn't going to change
I am a Muslim, that isn't going to change
Also Somali, that isn't going to change either
Young men and women equipped with nicknames so they may fit in society
Why be different when we are special, like M&Ms we come in different varieties

MLK had a dream, I have a vision
Islam no one can fabricate this true religion
Things I can't escape

So much violence attacks us mentally
Shoot blacks ruling it accidentally
Step back and think
Don't blink

Find a different solution but no
It's not like that,
Police like the strap
Knock the black man's cap

I don't discriminate,
It's like Latin, Caucasian, Black, Arab, and Asian
Different colors but we all the same
Stand as one
Don't take one step take a ton

Me and you
Walk on two
People's mentality more sick than the flu
No more they and me
But stick together as we

Streets getting colder
Cops getting bolder
People who fought for my rights getting older
I'mma take place in the game, call me an awoken soldier

Ama waa la muuqdaa ama waa la maqanyahay.

BE SEEN OR BE ABSENT.

SARA OSMAN

foreigner.

i am from sharp tongues and hushed voices.
from a people who squeeze me in such a tight embrace,
their warmth is imprinted on my soul.

it is lonely here.
this cold is unnatural.

i am from my Hooyo's shaah iyo uunsi
and her sly looks with an easy smile.
the simple chaos of Saturday mornings as we gather.
family is the soundtrack to my happiness.
love is easy to give here but hard to swallow.

i am from a place where i am forever reminded
that blood on the pavement looks a lot like paint on a canvas.

i think i called him brother . . . once?
now,
he is the dirt in the left quadrant of this cemetery.

i say my prayers into the ground next to him
as i dig my own grave.

i am from the land.
we are from the land.

we have always belonged to her.
    even when she abandoned us.

a home we struggle to remember but memories we are fighting to forget.

    here, we are growing in between the cracks
    our tears serve as fertilizer.

        look how we make things grow,
        like makeshift alchemists,
        crafting a life out of nothing.

           have we not yet earned our redemption?

this.
this is all i have.

    what i am.

i want to stay.
but this is so far from where my grandmother's bones sleep,

      i worry God won't find me here.

Shimbirba shimbirkiisu
la duulaa.

BIRDS OF A FEATHER
FLOCK TOGETHER.

AISHA MOHAMED

Who Am I?

I love when it is dark
I love it when it is dark
everything is peaceful and quiet
I love the darkness of the night
when no one can see me crying or smiling
you might only see the shape of my body, not my feelings

I'm an emotional person who cries easily
Remembering my childhood
I cry
when I remember
the green and red bruises
Awoken with a beating
for money that went missing always
blamed
I'm the kind of person who doesn't show her feelings
but at the same time there is something that's burning inside me

When I was in Somalia, my homeland, I grew up without a mom and a dad
a pain only someone who has tasted it can understand

My mom left us when we were little so she could give us the perfect life we deserve
my dad couldn't provide, I don't blame him he had no wealth
Every time someone says *dad*, I feel sad he didn't raise us
stayed a father, not a dad
never protected us from my aunt
never there when we needed him

Mom waited alone in Egypt for her chance to come to America,
she did finally come to America,
a blessing from Allah that
changed our life.
Long-awaited reunion,
in America I can be beside her
I can get a good education in America
my mother sacrificed to give us a better life
that even my dad couldn't give us

ALI ALI

The Metallic Star

I have the diseased and the poor,
frivolously I wait with nothing to adore,
it's equivalent to hell, but without a course,
no shelters in sight, no birds that soar,
it's a deserted place with devils at core,
perhaps no man's land was just a thorn,
to the problems that have just been born.
Bloodlust awaits, because clans are at war.

But without the peace, and guns at hand,
they attack each other with their sons in bands,
some three years old, sadly some are one,
a loss is a loss, nothing can be done,
there are no chances given to the losing side,
they must abide by the winner's whim or stagger till they die.
This heartfelt story makes you cry, knowing it's true, you begin to cry.

Even the rich are poor,
with no water to store,
no rain in sight, no droplets on the floor,
I am dead in heat, no crops to eat,
dreaded in sweat left to die, and yet . . .
we continue living as if nothing happened.
So thank God almighty, and you may go to heaven.

This is Somalia, this is me.
With no peace in sight, I'll never be seen.

AHMED SHAIKH

One-Man Team

I'm a Somali
Arab with a dream,
a one-man team,
independent person.

They say blacks are thugs and killers.
I am not
They treat all Arabs like terrorists
I am not a terrorist

I am a person with a dream to support his family to make my mother happy
And thank her for everything she did for me
Tucked me in bed each night
Fed me when I was hungry
Kept me warm when I was cold.

But if people want to keep treating me like a terrorist,
I will stand up for myself to speak my truth until the end
It feels like a war zone, a mortal combat, street fighting
Oh, my God, this feels like a life sentence in this place
If money grew on trees, I would climb up and rest in it
Build a treehouse and knock the bird nest out
I want to bail out, powering up like power troopers.
Knock these haters out like Ali.

Ammin dumay dib uma soo laabto.

LOST TIME IS NEVER FOUND AGAIN.

HIBAQ MOHAMED

ABOUT WORDS UNWRITTEN

This is a prose poem about the power of securing one's narrative in written form. I come from the Somali culture, where oral language is valued more, so it was easy growing up to value the unwritten words just as much as the written. Of course, as an adult and educator, it has become more and more evident that the only way to secure one's narrative in the dominant society is through the written word.

This piece is about the transition to accepting the written word. It is called "Words Unwritten" and looks closely at the internal struggles of trying to capture one's words. The beginning of the poem talks about the speaker's internal struggles to secure all that is within. As the poem continues, the speaker reflects on the historical triumphs that took place to create the written Somali language. As the poem comes to an end, the speaker finds a way to capture what is within through the written word while still valuing the spoken.

The poem also discusses the barriers of words when trying to capture the language of the mind. For people who speak multiple languages, it is often a challenge to get those thoughts on paper when the words refuse to come.

I want readers to know the struggle of bilingual students and understand that sometimes they have more to say than meets the eye.

HIBAQ MOHAMED

Words Unwritten

I was never the type who wanted to write, but my mind spits words a world away and there is little time to capture it in any other way. So, I try to write.

In the dark night, when the day settles and the hustle takes a rest, my mind begins to uncover all that has been done. It unfolds the mysteries of the day and in the only way I know. I capture it all. So, I begin to write.

My forefathers were men of words. I was told my grandfather fought wars of words. Making sense of letters into visual images, desperately trying to convey meaning through carved images, tasked with capturing centuries of words before words were even written. So, he wrote and rewrote. He discussed it over tea with local men, and they tried to make sense of it all. So, they wrote.

As I write, I am reminded of my ancestral mind—as it throws a thousand images of words yet to be discovered. I am tormented to write with the few existing words, which give no real way of capturing it all. So, filled between the lines lie words left behind. That I am destined to write.

My desire to capture it all is often interrupted by thoughts I cannot put down. Lost words force their way onto paper. Yet I cannot write them. Each word desperately trying to make it to the finish line. And so, desperately, I write.

PART III

CARRYING THE DREAM, DEFYING THE ODDS

ASMA AHMED

Shifting Gears

Like me, most in the Somali diaspora grew up in communities where Soomaalinimo enticed a bitter laugh that echoed in our ears. The echoes grew louder with time, and eventually we all began to face contradicting dualisms in different facets of life. It seemed like we were always charting a new path, breaking boundaries, raising the glass ceiling, and adding to a narrative that didn't want to include us. We kept trying to fit in, and some of us succeeded, but most of us sat on the benches waiting for our turn to play. I too was waiting for that chance to finally be understood by my white peers and my Somali community. The dichotomy of my story was always there: too Somali to be American and too American to be Somali—and then there was the part of me that spent five years of my childhood in Damascus, Syria, making me the "Carabiyad" among my Somali American friends. I consider it a bitter blessing to have remained on the bench long enough to realize I could create my own team and play on my own time. The courage to chart my own path was bred in me by my mother, whose recurring catchphrase has always been "waa iisiy." *Easy*. It can be the craziest idea, but no matter how offset I was, Hooyo would always reassure me and push me further towards my dreams—especially in moments of doubt.

My mother grew up in a household where her mom was the breadwinner, and as the eldest daughter, my mother was hooyo labaad, a second mom, to her siblings. There was a sense of tenacity and urgency in her upbringing that drove her to excel academically. Back in those days, education in Somalia was free but selective; only a handful of applicants were allowed to continue at each level. My mom was proudly among the few selected for a pre-med track. Unfortunately, the civil war put an abrupt halt to her studies. But her passion and high aptitude for STEM education remained and trickled down to us.

My journey in STEM was adventurous, to say the least. I had always been curious about how things work and how innovation and scientific understanding can be leveraged to raise the standard of living for people across the globe, but I didn't know what path to take to satiate this curiosity. My indecisiveness led me to mechanical engineering, a major viewed as the jack-of-all-trades in STEM. I quickly became involved with multiple project-based student organizations and tried to acquaint myself with classmates and professors in the department. I remember feeling insecure and misplaced, especially when I realized no amount of code-switching was *ever* going to be enough to ground me. I was different, and I had to accept that.

A mechanical engineering professor gave me some golden advice that helped me reconcile the dualisms in my life: personalize systems around you and use your diversity as your strength. Two years ago, I didn't fully understand what he meant, but now I can clearly see how my intersectional identity is my competitive edge.

My ability to tap into resources from multiple communities gave me direct access to greats like Elman Ahmad, Hawo Tako, Sayid Abdulle Hassan, Malcolm X, Imam Shamil, and Omar bin Abdul Aziz. I see myself as an indirect product of their sacrifices. Today, their stories, along with my mother's, are the fuel that ignites my academic and professional ventures. So instead of rushing to play a game that has already started, I stand beside that same bench, dribbling my own ball, recruiting a different set of players, and patiently waiting for a new game to start.

SARA OSMAN

roots.

i think i saw my own death once.
    felt the air leave my lungs
    the soul leave my body
but it is a faded memory now
i think i was buried alive
they thought that if i ate the dirt here,
maybe the land would accept my body
instead, i became the conduit for new life
reimagined my legs as trees,
my skin as bark
crafted the river as my hair
my laughter like the wind
here,
i am growing
and
growing
and
growing
    uninterrupted.
        let your prayers for me be carried by the breeze
        tell my people that i have made it home
            safely.
                finally.

Af daboolan dehab.

SILENCE IS GOLDEN.

NASRA ABDIMALIK

Through My Mind

Do you know what comes through my mind?

They say we are all equal in life, but I ask, "Are we really?"

"Hello, neighbor!", "Beautiful day!", or "Hey, you can sit next to me."

Our number-one rule has become nothing but beautiful rainbows and equality.

Our visions are dimmed due to the thought of a perfect utopia.

But see, in reality we are discriminating against everyone for who they are and what they stand for. No one's perfect. And no one ever was in this world.

A Muslim person cannot go out without being terrorized. Who is the terrorist?

They could ask, "What culture are you?" or even construct questions like, "What led you to wear this clothing?" because such questions would gain them knowledge, like how non-Muslims from Europe wore headscarves way before we walked the face of the earth. But do they ever ask such questions? The answer is no. Instead, they ask things like, "What's on your head?", "Can't you take it off?", "Isn't it too hot?", or "Why is your outfit so long and abnormal?" Does it feel okay to show all your skin? I ask. Do you feel shame, I wonder?

Those words really get to us so much that we just start to believe there's something wrong with our traditions and beliefs. Nothing can be wrong with our traditions and beliefs!

As Muslims who live in America, we are starting to lose our culture and what we believe in.

We are so brainwashed and led to think we are supposed to live up to what the Americans think a Somali should do or be. And that is truly wrong!

It's like we've lived a lie all our lives.

We should remember we are Soomaali who live in America.

We are the generation that could risk letting our Somali culture die.

This lie we are all living aren't getting us anywhere in life.

We cannot lose who we are, our hope in our Somali culture.

A culture that should be remembered in America or wherever we are as Somali.

The Somali culture is unique and should be preserved.

Otherwise our language will be forgotten and our traditions will be lost forever.

We are the future generation, and it is time for us to show pride in who we are; to bring back to life our unique culture and show the world its true beauty, the beauty our ancestors once gracefully showed.

LEYLA SULEIMAN

I Am Somali/Soomaali Baan Ahay

With his deep, smooth voice, my father sang verses of old songs that reflected the joys of his childhood in Buuloberde. Like my Ayeeyo, his mind collects poetry, songs, proverbs, and stories; through the words of Somali poets and the stories of our people, he invites me into the powerful, joyful, wise world he knows to be Somalia—though, to many, this Somalia no longer exists. He taught me the legendary poem "Soomaali Baan Ahay" by Abdulkadir Hersi Siyad (Yamyam).

"In these relentless days,
if you have been truly alive,
reflect on past times,
trace back the lines,
ask yourself:
Who is Somali?"
Soomaali baan ahay. I am Somali.

The poem speaks of the pride and fearlessness of the Somali legacy, yet the question it demands I ask—who is Somali?—fills me with a sad longing. I want to stand up and say with confidence, I am Somali! And oftentimes when I am confronted with the question by other Somalis—not *who* but *what* are you?—that is exactly how I reply.

"What are you?"

"I am Somali." I am met with a blank look that eases quickly into a confused half smile, like they are ready to laugh and are simply waiting for the punch line.

I wait a while. I let them run through different regions and clans in their mind, thinking about different boxes that it would be comfortable to put me in.

"Are you sure you're Somali?"

I laugh and say, "What do you mean? Of course I'm sure." Then, sometimes, I will ease their confusion with one of the first Somali phrases I learned: "Aabbahay waa Soomaali, hooyadayse waa Cadaan." *My dad is Somali, my mom is white.*

Relief washes over their face as they make sense of me.

"Soomaali Baan Ahay" is a poem that should leave me with the urge to run to a hilltop and wave the Somali flag for all the world to admire. Or fly back to Galdogob and lie in the bright red sand until my heart realizes it is finally home. And when I am content to be wholly myself, sitting alongside my Somali father and my Norwegian mother and never torn between them, the pride of that poem rushes through my veins. It is only when I am tempted to view myself through the ever-sorting minds of others that "Soomaali baan ahay!" becomes "Soomaali baan ahay?"

But when the doubt begins to overwhelm me and I question where I belong, I trace back my lines. I am a daughter of nomads and vikings who were free and proud and strong. And so I give myself permission to embrace it all. To be neither and both. To never choose.

ILHAAN ABDIKARIM

A Blue World, with a Single Star

Red, white, and blue
Made from thread that could fly even if the wind is light
Not a task, thought, not even a single clue
Of how it means to be so bright

Red, white, and blue
Made from soft cotton
Upon the pole
Where people salute

My language
The beauty
The horror and pain
From the story, I've been told
To be a doctor someday

The thought of being the future
Of this cruel, cruel world
Gets me giddy
Excited to the core
Of making the world better
As it once was before humans started to actually think

Earplugs on
And face turned away
Independence is key
For kids my age

Kids my age wear plastic smiles
Speak with the sudden informality
And become like everyone else
They are all the same

Why aren't you tired?
Of being reminded of who you are
When you know yourself better than anyone
Except they could describe you more than you can count

Red, white, and blue is the world you have to love
You look around and feel your heart beginning to sink
Depression forming, tears blurring your vision
Trickling down your cheeks
Holding yourself tight
Because the only person is here with you
who haunts you, who hates you and loves you
who will never leave you behind
Is you
All because you don't know what world you live in

I'm not unique
Just utterly different
I'm not the gift from the Nile
I sometimes think I'm no gift at all

Opened hair
And Bluetooth blast
The streets of the urban

My home at last
I belong to the blue world with a single star
But why can't I say it, shout it, cry it all out?
Why am I envious of those who love and know themselves?
Who love and know everyone else
Who love and know what world they are surrounded in

I'll give you a message,
From a meek young girl
Who knew the basics of her language
Broken and still

Went to her mother's home
Her father's birthplace,
Where families are happy, not misplaced
She then passed the people with the memorable scars
Her very one and only absolute mistake

Everyone could see the pity in her eyes
The place she called home is where she was distanced,
People wouldn't recognize her from across the street
Unfamiliar of her name, her father's name, or who she is
She was a world full of red, white, and blue

I wouldn't call it special
But it's one of a kind
When you leave your protective shell
What could be in your mind?

The stares, the looks
Wherever you are
The confidence should arise
But some just hide away in the murky shadows beneath them
And one of them is me

The thing is for being different
You'll feel like you're tested
The thing is for being different
You'll feel like you're all alone

I know, after an endless search, I will never belong
But I have a life in this world
The red, white, and blue
But I couldn't tell if it's the truth

I'm a girl you won't see every day
Be a stranger with a different thought
At least you've got a guessing game to play
Whenever you look at me in the eyes
My plain, dark, empty, lifeless eyes

Red, white, and blue
Made from thread that could fly even if the wind is light
Not a task, thought, not even a single clue
Of how it means to be so bright

Red, white, and blue
Made from soft cotton
Upon the pole
Where people salute

I live in a world with red, white, and blue
But my heart and soul belongs
To the blue world with a single star

Guri aan hooyo lahayni waa lama degaan.

A HOME WITHOUT A MOTHER IS EMPTY.

FAIZO ABDI MOHAMED

Sheekadayda, Xusuustayda

For English translation, see page 83.

Waxaan xasuustaa maalin anoo socoto ah. Waxaa da' ayay roob aad u badan. Waxaan ku jiray jawi aad u qurux badan. Waxaa iisoo dhacay teleefoonkii aan watay! Waxaa isoo wacay Aabbaheey, wuxuu ii sheegay inaan soo aado Addis ababa, kadibna aan ka sii aadi doono wadanka Mareeykanka. Runtii waxay ii ahayd farxad lama filaan ah balse hadana waxaa garab socday inaan ka tagayo hooyadeey macaan, walaalahay iyo sidoo kale magaaladii aan ku dhashay ee Baladweyn. Waxaan u socday abbaheey oo aan in mudo ah arkin iyo walaaladay oo aan waligay arkin. Maalmo kadib waxaan u soo ambab-axnay aniga iyo walaasheey farhxia wadanka Ethiopia gaar ahaan magaalada Adis ababa waxaan halkaas joognay mudo sannad ah kadibna waxaan uga soo anba baxnay dalka Maraykanka. Waxaan kusoo dagnay magaalada Washington, DC, waxaan halkaas transit ku ahayn mudo lix saacadood ah, kadibna diyaarad kale ayaa naga soo qaaday waxaana soo gaarnay magaalada Minneapolis ee gobolka Minnesota waxaa garoonka nagu soo dhaweeyay Aabbahay Cabdi Jimcaale iyo Eedaday Nimco Rooble,

Adeerkey Axmed Jimcaale iyo eedadeey Xakiima, dhamaan walaaladay iyo sidoo kale dhamaan qoyskeena. Aabbahay wuxuu ahaa mid raadiyo farxadeena wax kastoo aan rabno ayuu noo samayn jiray. Aabbaheey waxuu iiga sheekeeyay markii uu imaaday wadd-ankan Maraykanka waxii uu kala kulmay sida uu ku bilaabay shaqadii ugu horaysay iyo dhamaan shaqooyinkii uu soo qabtay oo runtii ahaa kuwo aad u dhib badan, waxuu kasoo shaqeeyay gobolo kala duwan oo waddankaan ah. Intaas oo dhib ahna wuxuu u maraayay sidii aan anaga horumar u gaari lahayn. Ugu danbayn wuu gaaray himiladiisii ahayd in ilmahiisa ay wax u bartaan kuna noolaadaan farxad iyo nabad galyo. Aniga mudadii aan aabbahay kala maqnayn mar kasto aniga booska aabbo wuu iga maqnaa xilligii aan joogay Soomaaliya. Marka aan la ciyaarayo ilmaha waxaan dareemi jiray in abbaheey iga maqan yahay laakiin isaga rafaad badan ayuu u soo maray in aan farxad helno. Laakiin hadda waa mid naga buuxiyay dhinacii aabbanimo. Hadda waxaan ahay gabar la nool abbaheed wa-laalaheed iyo qoyskeeda, laakiin waxaan mar kasta xasuustaa sidii wanaag sanayd ee ay hooyaday iisoo barbaarisay oo runtii aan qoraal lagu soo koobi Karin.

Qof walboow xasuusnoow qiimaha ay hooyo leedahay. Hooyo waa lafdhabarka bani aadamka, hooyo waa qofka ugu samirka badan, uguna dulqaadka badan. Hooyo waa qofka ugu qadarinta badan, uguna xushmada. Badan hooyo waa qof intaba ilaahay ugu deeqay. Hooyo ma ahan mid xaqeeda la gudi karo dhamaan. Hooyooyinkeen ilaahay janada guri ha ugu dhiso. Waxaan kaloo u xiisay dalkeeygii hooyo iyo meshaan kusoo koray Baledweyne. Sidoo kale markii aan waddankaan imaaday waxaa igu adkaatay la qabsiga nolosha. Wadankaan waxaan dareemay inaan joogo waddan shisheeye. Waxaa igu adkaatay inaan ku hadlo luqada. Waxaanse i caawin jiray walaalkeey iga yar, Moxamed oo mar kasto iga caawin jiray wax kasto oo aan is lee yahay caawimaad ayaad uga baahan tahay dhinaca wax barashada. Sidoo kale waxaa mar kasto garabkeeyga ka marnaan jirin abaheeyga, Alle ha ii daaye wuxuu ahaay mid garabkeeyga taagan xili kasto, wuxuu ahaay aabbo midka ugu fiican ee dunida si kastabo wax yaabaha layaabka igu ahaa waxaa ka mida barafka iyo qaboowga halkaan ka jira iyo markii la gaaro xiliga kulaylka oo hadana ah mid aanan horay usoo arag. Waxaan dareemi jiray inaa kasoo tagay waddan aan is badalin hawadiisa, waxaa dareemi jiray inaa kasoo tagay waddan leh qeeyraad fara badan, waxaan mararka qaar xasuusan jiray markii aan soo aado suuqa, waxaan isa soo raaci jirnay saxibteeydii aan jeclaa, Xaawo Luul. Markaan midig iyo bidix fiiriyo waxay ahayd mid garabkayga taagan. Xaawo luul waxeey aheed saaxiib igu qaali ah oo aan marna hilmaami karin inta aan noolahay. Waxaan ku wada noolayn hal magaalo oo ah Beledweyn dadka magaaladaas dagan waxay noogu yeeri jireen mataanihii xaafada Dhagax-jibis. Markii aan imid waddankan Maraykanka waxaa la i geeyay iskool. Waxaana halkaas iska baranay saaxiibteeyda labaad oo lagu magacaabo Saynab. Saynab waa gabar aad u dabeecad wanaagsan, dhan kasto waana saaxiibta kaliya ee aan ku leeyahy waddankan Maraykan-ka. Saynab waxay igula nooshahay magaalada Rochester, gobolka Minnesota. haddii aan dib ugu laabto xasuustaydii Soomaaliya iyo dalkan Mareykanka waa labo waddan oo kala duwan, waa laba waddan oo kala dhaqan ah, waa labo waddan oo xagga luqada ku kala duwan. Waxaan Soomaaliya uga imid dad isku af ah, isku midab ah, isku dhaqan ah, iskuna diin ah, laakiin Mareeykanka waxaan ugu imaaday dad kala midab ah, kala diin ah, kala af ah, kala dhaqan ah, leh boqolaal dhaqan oo kala duwan. Waxaan dareemaa haddii aan ahay gabar Soomaaliyeed, muslimad ah oo ku nool dalka Mareeykanka, in aan u dhax-eeyo labo waddan oo kala dhaqan gadisan. Hadda waxaan ahay ardayad dhigato schoolka Rochester Stem Academy. Waxaan ahay gabar jecel dhaqankeeda, dalkeeda iyo diinteeda. Waxana ku faani jiray calankeena buluuga ah ee xiddigta cad, ee shanta gees leh dhaxda uga taal waana ku faani doonaa inta aan noolahay nolosheeyda.

Sirow ma hodmo.

A DECEIVER NEVER PROSPERS.

FAIZO ABDI MOHAMED

My Story, My Memory

I remember one day as I was traveling, it rained hard. I was feeling good and my telephone rang! It was my father. He told me to come to Addis Ababa and that I would eventually be traveling to the United States. This was truly an unexpected pleasant surprise. At the same time, I understood that I would be leaving behind my dear mother, siblings, and my hometown of Beledweyne.

Soon, I traveled with my sister to Addis Ababa and on to my father, whom I had not seen for a long time, and my siblings, whom I had never seen. We stayed in Addis Ababa for a year.

Then we landed in Washington, DC. We stayed at the airport in transit for six hours. We took another plane and landed in Minneapolis, Minnesota. We were met at the airport by my father, Cabdi Jimcaale, as well as my aunt Nimco Rooble, uncle Axmed Jimcaale, aunt Xaliimo, and all my siblings. My father always worked hard to make us happy so we could do everything we wanted.

My father told me about when he came to the United States and had his first job. He did a few different odd jobs, and some were quite difficult. He also lived in a few states. He did that so he could help us succeed. He finally reached his goal of getting an education for his children and living in peace and happiness.

The time my father and I were separated, I used to miss him—especially when I played with other kids and their fathers. But that whole time, he was working hard to get us reunited and make us happy. I am now a girl who lives with my father, my siblings, and my entire family. I will always remember the excellent way my mother raised me. There were more good things than I can put in writing.

I want everyone to know how important a mother is to raising a child. A mother is the backbone of humanity, the most patient and most forgiving. A mother truly cares and respects. God put all these qualities in a mother's heart. I can never repay my mother for the things she has done for me. May Allah build a house for all moms in heaven.

I am homesick for Beledweyne, the place I grew up in, and my home country. At the same time, when I came to this country, I had a hard time adjusting to life in the United States. I felt I was a foreigner, and had trouble speaking the language. I got a lot of help from my younger brother, Mohamed, who is always willing to help me with everything I need help with in school. My father has always been on my side as well, and may Allah give him a long life. He is the best father anyone can ask for.

Minnesota's weather is very unusual to me, and it took some time to get used the cold, the snow, and the summer heat. I went from a land where the weather is the same to a land where the weather changes.

One of my favorite memories is going to the local market with my best friend, Xaawo Luul. She was always with me everywhere we went. She is a friend I will never forget. We lived together in Beledweyne, in a part of town called Dhagax-Jibis. We were known as the twins of Dhagax-Jibis.

When I came to the United States, I started school. There I met Saynab, my best friend in this country. Saynab is a girl who is easy to get along with. She is the only friend I have in the United States. She lives in Rochester, Minnesota, with me. The United States and Somalia are very different, two different cultures and languages. In Somalia, people speak the same language, have the same culture and the same religion, and are the same race. In the United States, people speak different languages, have different cultures, have different religions, and are of different races.

Alif kaa xumaaday Albaqra kaama haro.

ONE DOES NOT THRIVE ON A
WEAK FOUNDATION.

AISHA MOHAMED

Who Am I? Part 2

What do I mean, I love darkness?
Loving darkness means to me so much.
I can hide my feelings, my tears, and my weakness.
I used to hide almost every day.
Life taught me so many lessons
That made me who I am and
Brought me to where I am today.
My tears taught me how to be brave,
My weakness taught me how to keep going,
My feelings taught me how to breathe again,
My heartbeat taught me that there is hope.
Hope—with every single heartbeat that comes from my heart.
My silence is full of answers, and
Allah made me who I am
Which is a huge blessing.
I will be successful in the future, and
End up somewhere good.
No matter how hard it is, I will try.

QALI ABDI

Dhulka Dhexe (Middle Ground)

"Where are you from?" The question always created conflict for me. You would ask my parents or grandparents the question and there would be no hesitation before "Beledweyne" or "Somalia" tumbled from their mouths. All my other siblings were born in America and would answer nonchalantly with "Mankato" or "Eagle Lake," maybe even "Minnesota," without any thought. I, however, have put *plenty* of thought into it. Too much thought, perhaps.

My parents brought not only clothing to America but also a suitcase full of stories. My parents open that story suitcase to recall childhood memories about their hometown of Beledweyne, Somalia. A part of me desperately wants to relate to their memories, like when they talk about the vastness of the jungle that surrounds the Shebelle River or the camels my grandpa herds. No matter how hard I try, I can scarcely identify with any of their stories. I might have been born in Somalia, but that is where my story suitcase ends. I brought no memories with me, because I immigrated to the US at the age of two. Essentially, I was raised in the small city of Mankato, Minnesota.

I spent the early years of my life in a blue three-bedroom apartment. I lived without a care in the world, as many children do. My family loved that blue apartment because the complex radiated love as well as comfort. Our neighbors were mostly Somali families, along with other people of color. We lived happily, until my parents dropped the sentence "We're moving." Then we had to say goodbye to our haven.

My cultural perception was not a perplexing matter when I moved. Nobody questioned that I was Somali. It just never occurred to me that I was American too. I was me, Qali. But then I started at the local elementary school. Only two other Somalis attended Eagle Lake Elementary, and they just so happened to be my siblings. Every time someone asked me, "Where are you from?" and I answered with the small town I had moved from, they would shake their head like a bobblehead, releasing the wretched words: "No, where are you *really* from?" That question had an emphasis on it that made me feel an outsider. Elementary school became the start of that question floating around everywhere I went.

During the fourth grade, differences arose with some of my classmates. Anyone with eyes could see the distinction between us. My classmates were all white, while I was black. My peers would often talk about a barbecue they had on the weekend or going up north to their cabin over a school break. Barbecue to me was a sauce, and I could not wrap my head around why you needed a second home. New differences came to light all the time. I found the dissimilarity humiliating. How could I be American if I could not relate to anything people around me enjoyed? The answer, for me, lay in my Somali culture.

Daily, I would find a new aspect to hate at home. I would ask my mom, "Hooyo, why do you cook bariis [rice cooked with goat meat and spices] or baasto [pasta with home-made sauce] every day?" or "Hooyo, why do we only have anjaro [sour pancakes, sort of like the Ethiopian Injera but sweeter] or malawah [sweet, thin pancakes] for breakfast?" I wanted to have takeout and Pop-Tarts, as the kids on TV had for dinner and breakfast. All characteristics of my culture bothered me. It seemed almost wrong to be me when every-one else was not.

A small fire of self-hatred started inside me, and it grew as I gained friends who did not have the same culture as me. One time, my childhood friend Rachel saw my dad in his macawis (a long cloth worn around the waist, similar to the East Asian lungi) taking out the trash. We were playing outside one day, and she asked, "Why does your dad wear a skirt?" That sentence caused my face to flush. Is that what my dad's macawis looked like to her? Is that what everyone else saw? I had never perceived a macawis as a skirt until then. Rachel never asked about my dad's macawis again, but her words left a lasting impression on me for years.

Over the next few months, my hate for Somali culture became embarrassment. "Why me?" grew into the only question I wanted an answer to. If I'd had a chance to put everything about my culture in a jar and hide it the darkest corner of my closet, I would have. Of course, being in a dominantly white school, questions about my background were continually asked by parents or teachers. I would try my best to dodge them or try to make it seem like I knew barely any information about my culture. Always trying to hide my identity was exhausting. I was running a race that had no finish line. My dream of being normal seemed impossible. All I wanted to do was not be different from my peers, yet here I was, about as different as one could be. It was not until I finished elementary school that my self-awareness started to change.

Although it took many years, I eventually accepted I was Somali. This was a reality that could not be changed. It was revolutionary, progressive growth for me. I may not have completely cherished or loved my culture yet, but a more tolerant feeling floated around the topic. This acceptance of myself made me more curious about my roots. The more questions I asked about my culture, the less hatred surrounded it. I practiced my Af-Soomaali (the Somali language) daily at home, slowly trying to read it too. Hooyo taught me culinary aspects of Somali culture, including how to cook baasto and bariis. My grandma bought me dozens of colorful baatis (traditional cotton housedresses). Every time I learned something, a new piece of me was unlocked. At long last, I felt content with myself.

During my ninth-grade year, my friend group changed and grew. I made more friends who looked like me. They wore hijabs and long maxi skirts and were as Somali as could be. I cannot find words to explain how comforting it is to discover individuals who comprehend things you have experienced. My mouth was sore and tired of explaining things, so I found people who were not expecting an explanation. There was hardly any conflict or contention in this bunch until the topic of grades came up one day. I was proud of myself, so I decided to show them my grades. I remember one friend scrolling down the grades on the computer as she told me, "Qali, you're *such* a white girl." At the time, I laughed it off, hiding my confusion. Should I have taken that as an insult or compliment? My friend took a pencil and erased the Somali part of me, the part I had worked so hard to discover. Unfortunately, this not the first time I'd had to hear that saying.

A major dilemma surfaced to me. In the Somali community, I am considered American. Aunts and uncles would tease me about how Af-Soomaali sounded on my tongue. "Maxaad u barawaysay afkaaga?" they would constantly ask. *Why have you not learned your language?* While Af-Soomaali flowed easily from their tongue, the language felt heavy and unfamiliar on mine. Going back and forth from two languages became an endless roller coaster. Another problem prevailed when I realized some words do not exist in another language. My brain turned into two distinct dictionaries. I was ripping pages, trying to flip through both of them ceaselessly. English in public, Af-Soomaali at home. Repeat. This cycle should have been easy. What kind of person struggles with their own language?

Whenever anyone talked about Somalia, I experienced a longing. I want to call it homesickness, but how could that be? I only lived there for two years before leaving. Ayeeyo constantly talked about the beautiful weather in Beledweyne, how you could pick gum from the xabag—not like American gum, but sap from the myrrh plant—and the year-round sweetness of fresh mango or guava. My parents and grandparents alike compared life in America with Somalia. I couldn't take part in these conversations, because I had nothing to compare. These discussions usually ended with a feeling of hopelessness.

At the end of the day, no culture had a bigger place in my heart. I perceived myself as too Somali for Americans, and not Somali enough for Somalis. In the middle of these two dissimilar cultures was me. No map could lead me to the place I belonged. The internal struggle of trying to discover words to identify with caused me to drift away from both cultures, until one day when I stumbled upon excerpts of poetry that talked about the difficulty of being part of a diaspora and how it seems you are being rejected from both cultures. Every word they wrote felt as though they stole the words out of my mouth and wrote them on paper. I finally felt understood.

Stumbling upon poetry books led me to other poets who went through cultural obstacles. Poetry had opened up a brand-new world. Barnes & Noble quickly became my favorite place to spend my afternoons. It felt as though the authors were addressing me face-to-face. The more I read, the more clarity came with the topic of cultural identification. The storm of clashing thoughts of self-hate had stopped. The sun had finally come out.

After getting into poetry, my mindset changed. There was no side to choose. I am Somali American. Waves of anger, confusion, and hurt that were tied to culture washed away. I am no surfer; there is no urgency to ever ride those waves again. I like to think the thoughts disappeared into the Atlantic Ocean. Much the same as me, the Atlantic is in the middle of the two nations that created me.

Ayeeyo was doing my hair one day while describing the small white house I was born in. As she tugged and pulled my hair into braids, I imagined that house and she recounted the day I came into the word. Ayeeyo was on my last braid when she said, "Waad arki doontaa guriga markaan uu laabano." *You will see the house when we go back.* That sentence created a sense of peace. I would go back one day.

Someday, I hope to adventure into the forest that surrounds the Shebelle River and to experience a day of herding with my grandfather. I want to feel on my skin the weather that all my ancestors experienced, to chew some xabag, to taste fresh fruit like mango and guava. With more practice, Af-Soomaali will not feel foreign on my tongue anymore. Instead, the language will glide gracefully off it. I will go to Beledweyne to bring back multiple suitcases with me wherever I end up. No, not suitcases of clothes or souvenirs, but luggage full of memories. At last, I will be the one to tell stories.

I may want to go to Somalia, but I cannot forget about America. A big mistake I make continually is not empathizing enough with my parents. Not only was my childhood full of firsts for me, but it also included many firsts for them too. They are truly the embodiment of the American dream. Thanks to them, my childhood consisted of reruns of *Toy Story* and cheating my way through Monopoly, along with countless birthday celebrations. Hooyo went from being a second-grade dropout to owning her own day care. Aabbo is currently going to school to get his associate's degree. America, for my family, represents growth. My family may have started out as a small seed, but we are starting to sprout.

"Where are you from?" a coworker asked me one day during our break. A knowing smile fell on my lips before answering, "I was raised in Minnesota, but I was born in Somalia." No conflict, no overthinking. Combining the two places that created me in one sentence hosed down the fire of self-hate I had. The fire ignites occasionally, but no power is given to it. The spark fizzles into nothing.

Nin sabraa sed leh.

THROUGH PATIENCE,
GREAT THINGS AWAIT.

RODA ABDI

The Young Observer's New Life

In the neighborhood that the girl lives in, there is always an abundance of languages spoken, the smell of several dishes from around the world wafting through the air of the hallways of the apartment complex. On the top floor lives a small family that no one sees. It is said that the mother is a woman who speaks very few words. The four children are well-mannered and politely greet their neighbors because it is considered rude to walk past strangers, especially elders, without a greeting. The girl sometimes yearns for the outside world: the people, the noise, and the community garden, which is the only place the mother lets her children go. When the girl leaves, she feels as though it is the only opportunity to drink the world in, so she does.

This particular day, the woman next door comes in during the wee hours of the morning to ask for sugar, and the younger brother screams at the sister to get some. Mother, who doesn't like the noise, comes down the stairs and tells her children not to yell. When everyone is ready to go, Mother makes the children recite a prayer before leaving the house. The sun is shining bright, an exciting proposition in a state where it sometimes feels like the warm weather is a daydream rather than a phenomenon that actually happens every summer. Girl is particularly excited because after she and her mother and siblings visit the garden, she is getting her ears pierced.

The piercing parlor is a strange sight for children who don't go out very often. The man who is doing the deed has large, meaty hands and a toothy, straight grin, almost as though his teeth don't entirely fit his mouth. Girl is overwhelmed by the various sights of the parlor: the gently run-down room, the sulfur-metal smell of the jewelry, the woman trying to console her daughter who just got her ears pierced. After the woman collects her child, it is Girl's turn. The man promises it will take no more than a second, and it will prick a bit. Mother says in her soft voice that Girl is mature in ways other Americanized children are not, is not a girl who has been ruined despite never knowing her homeland. Mother brags about this every opportunity she gets. Girl is more enamored by the strange tool the man is using. She decides to look ahead and thinks about the two new purple studs that will be attached to her ears, the ones she chose out of an assortment of small stud earrings. What a strange rite of passage, Girl thinks. The noise is loud, but the piercing gun is precise and exact. Girl is now Girl with Two New Fake Amethyst Studs in Her Ears.

On the way home, the pain starts to set in. Now it feels as though Girl's ears have their own heartbeat. Mother tells Girl she is proud of her. Girl's ears begin to hurt in a way that feels like a dull headache. When they arrive at their apartment complex at the top floor, the family goes its separate ways again.

Father, who has just come in from a day of grueling physical labor, is sitting on the couch, oblivious to how his daughter is one step closer to becoming an adolescent; and afterward, a young woman; and finally, a person allowed to go into the Real World, as they all like to refer to it. Is the world inside the home any less real? Girl doesn't want to be a part of the Real World because Mother has warned about the dangers that lurk outside, especially for girls who aren't afraid. Girl just wants to exist among her siblings and parents in her tiny, cozy utopia. Many children her age are enamored with and enticed by the Real World's dazzling lights, skyscrapers that seem to go on for eternity, and the masses of people who are always going somewhere, regardless of what time of day it is. Father is now languidly sprawled on the couch; Girl thinks he looks funny, and his long figure resembles a lazy cat. Girl, who has just left the third grade, is struggling with her math. Father, whose only commitment as father he dutifully fulfills is bringing home money, is hellbent on his daughter learning how to add and subtract. Girl isn't interested in math and how the neat numbers always add up at the end. She *can* do math. Her skill level isn't being questioned here. Girl isn't interested in math. She prefers the stories her teacher reads to her, the stories about fantastical lands and dragons and bears who have homes like humans. All these stories make her imagination run wild and make Mother proud when Girl becomes the child in her class who reads the most books.

Father, however, is less willing to bend the rules and let Girl read. He wakes up from his nap and barks at Girl to get her homework, and Girl and Mother flinch at the noise, but Girl complies. Father says in his commanding voice that Girl needs to learn to do math because, unlike English, math is a universal language. He tries to explain to his daughter that Mother and Father might have struggled with their English when they first came, but the math Girl is learning and the math Father was learning are the exact same. Girl, who has noticed Mother is at the door eavesdropping, has decided she will go to the kitchen to pour Father some shaah, traditional Somali tea. Father is hellbent but, you see, Girl is clever. And quiet. Girl makes sure to give Father some tea and promises in a sickly sweet voice that she will improve. Father, who is pleasantly surprised his daughter has become compliant, kisses her on her forehead. Girl skips back to her room, throws her math folder underneath her bed, picks up the newest book the librarian has loaned to her—*Charlie and the Chocolate Factory*—and reads until her lids close and her world becomes a hazy slumber.

AASIA ABDIWAHAB

Who Am I?

Who am I?
I don't know
Or maybe I just don't want them to know
Those people
The ones who hate me
Because I'm Muslim
And they think I shouldn't be
Maybe they hate me because I'm black
And they're white
Or because I'm Somali
And they're American
But wait
I'm American too
But when I try and say that
They'll respond
Disgusted
You?
Yes
Me!
I am Somali
But I was born here
an American
There it is again
Disgusted face
That lacks knowledge
What does that mean?
It means that "I" too am American

Then they'll leave
Those are the people
The ones who are close minded
The ones who think they own the land
They are the ones who think they can label me
With the glare who think they can change me
Me?
No one can change me!
My essence is far beyond their grasp
No one can change me
Or my person
Not touchable
I know who I am
Ask me again
Glaring,
Me?
Who am I?
I'm a black Muslim
Who was born here
Yes, in America
I am Somali
And you know what else?
I am proud
I don't shrink
Because I have history and culture I am proud
Giving, caring, loving
Those looks of confusion
I have learned how to respond with pride—nothing less!

Sirow ma hodmo.

A DECEIVER NEVER
PROSPERS.

KHADIJA MOHAMED

Pearls of Wisdom

My name is Khadija Mohamed. I am fourteen years old, and I am a Muslim. I was born and raised in Minneapolis, Minnesota. I am a first-generation Somali American. My parents immigrated to America in 1993 to flee the civil war in Somalia. In their hearts, they have a dream, and I hope to carry out their dreams. I remember this one time my mom and I had a heart-to-heart talk about me and my future. I remember it so clearly because it is one of the most important conversations I've ever had.

"Khadija, please come down here!" my mom shouted at me from downstairs.

"Hooyo, I'm coming down right now," I replied. That day my mom and I were home alone. I thought she had called me to clean up the house, but I was wrong. It was something completely different. "Hooyo, I'm down. What did you need?"

"Oh, you're here already. Great," she responded.

"Mom, did you want me clean or something?" I questioned.

"No, I called you for something else today." Now I was creeped out. I wondered, *Did I do something at school?* "I called you down for something that's really important to me."

"What?"

"Your future is really important to me. I hold your and your siblings' futures really close to my heart."

"Okay, um, Hooyo. I don't really know what you're talking about."

"What I am trying to say is, you are a grown girl, and you're in high school. You really need to start to think about your future."

"Um, okay, Hooyo. But I'm only in ninth grade. I have plenty of time." I was so confused because this conversation came out of nowhere. I was only a couple months into high school. I didn't think we'd have this conversation until I was ending my sophomore year, at the earliest.

"It does not matter what grade you are, Khadija. Any time is a good time to think about the future. I know you might think it's hard because of the world we live in today, but if you put your mind to it, anything is possible."

"Hooyo, always know I'll try my best to succeed for myself and for you and Aabbo."

"I bring up the fact that it might be hard for you because so many people are counting on you, both this family and your family back home in Somalia. Everyone back home is counting on you and your siblings. You know I always tell them you or one of your siblings could be a doctor or an engineer or a teacher. Sometimes I even throw in a president. Do you know why I tell them that?"

"No, but I think you're gonna tell me anyway."

"Yes, I will. I tell them that because when they hear you guys could be a doctor or a teacher, it gives them hope. They need doctors and teachers back home. They need people who can help rebuild our country. I just want you to think about your future and how you will use it."

"Okay, Hooyo. I'll take your advice. Thanks for this talk."

"Good. Now, go get started on those dishes."

"How did I know you were gonna say that?"

JABRIL HASSAN

This I Believe

You want to know how I live being known as a Somali Muslim in America?
You want to know how I feel when someone tells my parents to go back to Somalia?
You want to know how I feel when I see all the racism on social media?
These are people making fun of us, but for what?
Sometimes I feel like we are cursed
Then things are made worse

People are cautious if you wear a hijab with a big purse
People think differently if you wear a khamiis and a backpack
Don't tell me this isn't true because these are my truths
I've seen the social experiments on YouTube
What these people see in us are their own fears
I watched a YouTube video just the other day
A Muslim man with a backpack sat by a lady and she moved away
I wondered what she was thinking
What her biases were, her own prejudices
"Oh, it's a Muslim guy, and I got afraid."
Like I know kids who don't want to wear a khamiis because they're ashamed
Blaming Muslims for terror attacks!
Banning people's lives
Terrorist! Who is the terrorist?

Infamous tweets
Making bad history
Everyone looking at Muslims differently
This is what I have to say to Muslims, so listen carefully
You aren't alone, there are people just like you all over the map
They want us to give up, they want us to snap
They don't want to see us rise and succeed
I know you can be whatever you believe
You just have to make a goal and achieve
Muslims are just like everyone,
If you can read, we can read
If you can see, we can see
If we try our best, success is guaranteed

We should live with love and passion, not hate and greed
When I see a Muslim janitor, it destroys me
Like I want Muslims to be the employers, not the employees
I want to see more people like Zayn Malik and Muhammad Ali

My mom told me, If you're not planning to go to college, don't talk to me
I know you guys are wondering who this could be
I'm someone who believes in who I am

I am faithful. I believe in Islam. I have a story to tell.
My mom taught me to get back up no matter how hard I fell
I was taught if I gave up it would be hell
I was taught to be the one that's followed, not the follower
I was taught to grind and be a warrior
I was taught to be the leader

I was taught if someone did good, I can do better
I was taught to never forget my religion and culture
I was taught to grip my faith harder than a gun gripped by a soldier
I was taught to be the one to feed my family
I was taught on Fridays to wear my beautiful khamiis
I was taught to talk to my elders respectfully
I was taught to show only love and empathy
To even my worst enemies
I was taught on weekends to go to dugsi

Where the beautiful and holy Quran is what we're supposed to read
I was taught to shine without any light
I was taught if anything was wrong to make it right
I was taught to never give up and always fight

I was taught not to leave this world without a name
I was taught my religion and culture are what I should claim
I was taught to beat things not by force but by brains
I was taught to love myself and not be ashamed

Don't tell me you know what I'm talking about, me and you aren't the same
My parents went through hell to come to America, we aren't the same
My parents saw things nobody should ever see, we aren't the same
You haven't been called a terrorist on Twitter, we aren't the same
You haven't been told go back to your country, we aren't the same
You haven't been racially slurred by people on Snapchat, we aren't the same
We aren't the same, I am unique
We aren't the same, this I believe

ZAMZAM AHMED

Honor

My name is Zamzam Ahmed, and I am a senior at Wellstone International High School, where I play soccer. I was born in Kenya, where my parents went after leaving Somalia. I lived there as a refugee, along with my nine siblings. In Africa, I walked one hour to go to school because there were no cars or buses available to get me there. Before I went to school, I had to go to dugsi to study the Quran. One day, my mother received a call from the International Organization for Migration (IOM), which provides services and advice to migrants, displaced persons, and refugees. They told my mom, "You and your family are going to America."

When my mother told me, I was happy! I knew I would start a new education. I loved to study. I was happy and surprised because I was coming to a place of which I knew nothing. Once I got here, everything changed. I am learning a new language. I don't have to walk an hour to school anymore. I am a senior this year, and next fall I will be entering college.

The most difficult thing I have ever done happened when I was eleven years old. My mom went to Somalia, and she left me and my two older sisters in Kenya with my dad. I continued in school. My grandfather, who was sick, was really important in my life. He lived in a place so far away from my home. I always tried to visit my grandfather, but I had no chance to visit him because I was really busy Monday to Friday and going to dugsi Saturday and Sunday.

My grandfather went to the doctor, who said they had to take him into Nairobi, the capital city of Kenya, to treat his leg and save his life. My grandfather and my dad, who was his oldest child, went together because my grandfather couldn't get up to get something to eat. On the bus to Nairobi, my grandfather died. I was really sorry he died before I was able to visit him because he was the only person who always told me I shouldn't give up and who hoped I would achieve my dream.

I strive to consistently speak the truth with compassion and honesty. For example, when I'm at work, people want me to be honest to my job. I want to do what makes people more confident, like telling the truth. I believe people will trust me if I am always telling them the truth. When I am at school and I have a lot of homework or practice tests, I don't have to say, "Oh, I will do it tomorrow because I have a lot of time to practice." I have to be honest with my educators and how I would perform at college to prepare for my life. I have to be honest with my teachers and my classmates if we are doing group work in order and add my opinion honestly so everyone believes me. I must respect my two parents too. That's part of being honest.

FARTUN MOHAMED

Making the Journey Worthwhile

My name is Fartun Mohamed. I am a wife, a mother, a nurse-midwife, and Somali.

I left Somalia at the age of five and traveled through East Africa to Saudi Arabia prior to moving to the place destined to be my home for the next seven years, San Diego, California. I arrived there with my family at the age of eleven. As a young girl, I was very ambitious as result of the constant reminder from my parents to be "better" by working hard in school and staying out of trouble in order to go further in life—an opportunity they didn't have. Seeing myself as a proud daughter and dealing with the dilemma of my youthfulness, I had internal struggles trying to fit into a new culture and new identity while maintaining a culture that I had a limited understanding of.

I decided to learn more about my background and my culture by taking interest in Somali history, food, clothing, and music. I started watching videos and looking at pictures of Somalia. I started having conversations with my parents and older relatives to help me gain a greater insight. Thankfully, I was successful with my mission. By the time I was a senior in high school, my Somali was decent and I, along with few other Somali students, had successfully organized our first Somali culture dance show to participate in the annual Multicultural Day.

After high school, I moved to Minnesota. Valuing education, my parents drilled it into my head to choose a career as a doctor. I didn't take that path, as it seemed long in my youthful mind. However, I knew I loved working with people, so I decided to try nursing. In the process, I earned my nursing assistant certificate. It allowed me to work with seniors, providing one-on-one care. I really enjoyed working with them as much as they enjoyed me. That inspired my goal to pursue nursing. In the midst of that pursuit, I met my supportive husband and continued through the program while becoming a mother. After completing my associate's degree, I went on to earn my bachelor's degree while raising my own family. Thirsty for more education, I decided to go back to school and successfully earned my doctorate of nursing degree in the midwifery specialty from the University of Minnesota.

Looking back, I am thankful for my parents' courage, dedication, and resilience. They were forced to flee their home and their land. My mother, growing up as an orphan, was very bright and talented. She managed to work, save money, and start her own family at the age of seventeen. She and my father have inspired and influenced me by shaping me into the woman I am today.

AMAL MOHAMED

Never Will I Be the Same

I will never be the same
I mean, for real, don't you see my name?

It's hard playing more than one role
But I guess it makes me a whole

I like considering myself half and half
But if I said it out loud, people would laugh

Can't I be considered both?
Or maybe I'm just Somali

Maybe I try so hard to fit in
Maybe it's the color of my skin

Why am I so different? It must be my race
Cause just like them, I grew up in this place

They say this is the land of the free
But sorry, I just don't agree

You see, growing up wasn't easy for me
I was never allowed to just be

Regular questions like, Why do I wear what I wear?
And I'd be rude if I asked, Why do you care?

So please object if you think this is fair
And when it comes to America, how do they dare say I don't care?

I mean, yes, I'm mad that my people are banned
But this too is my land

Maybe I will never look like you
But what can I do?

'Cause what I wear and how I speak
It makes me unique

And I won't disclaim my culture
Just to fit in another

So yeah, I don't have my name to blame
I just never will be the same . . .

Awrka danbe awrka hore saanqaad kiisuu leeyahay.

THE YOUNG CAMEL FOLLOWS THE FOOTSTEPS OF THE OLDER CAMEL.

Thank you to all the Somali storytellers,
past and present, who carry their stories
forward for future generations.

About the Editor

Marian A. Hassan (Ubah) spent her childhood loving language, listening to stories, and memorizing poetry and songs from the rich oral language of her native Somalia. These days, she still loves language, still listens to stories in all mediums, and finds joy in sharing the gift of books and stories with children and parents. She is the author of the bilingual children's books *Bright Star, Blue Sky* and *Dhegdheer: A Scary Somali Folktale*, as well as *The ABCs of Peace*, to be published by Red Leaf Press.

About the Authors

Time does not stand still and neither do our authors.
All bios are current as of the time that the pieces were originally submitted.

AASIA ABDIWAHAB was born in Minnesota and has lived here her entire life. She is a sophomore at Ubah Medical Academy. She loves to read, especially fantasies, and her favorite is the Harry Potter series.

AHMED SHAIKH enjoys games and writes about things he thinks about during the day but cannot say out loud in front of everyone.

AISHA MOHAMED was born in Somalia and came to the US on November 23, 2016. She is an outgoing girl who loves going to the gym and writing poetry to express her feelings.

ALI ALI attends Saint Paul College as a PSEO student through Step Academy, and has always been fond of poetry. Born in Minneapolis, Minnesota, he struggled to determine whether he'd become a writer or a poetic rapper. His first rap was designed to match Muhammad Ali's catchphrase, which he changed to, "I may charge like a rhino, while you scream like a donkey, if my fist doesn't faze you, what will is my mommy."

AMAL MOHAMED is a tenth-grader at Ubah Medical Academy. Even though Amal has never been to Somalia, she has always felt a connection to her country. Every chance she gets, she finds a way to learn more about the Somali culture and history. Amal joined the Somali anthology project to share her knowledge and curiosity of her country with other young Somali people.

ARDO MOHAMUD is a rising junior at Southwest High School. She grew up listening to her mother's poems and started to gain an interest in poetry. During her spare time, she loves watching Korean dramas. Ardo also enjoys cooking Somali food, because she learned how during her childhood. She likes reading genres such as nonfiction, fiction, and dystopian literature. She lives in south Minneapolis, Minnesota, with her parents, three sisters, and five brothers.

ASMA AHMED is a fourth-year mechanical engineering student at the University of Minnesota. She is passionate about economic development, community enrichment/education, and volunteerism. She plans for a career in the health care sector and is involved with a few East African NGOs. Her hope is to be among the Somali millennials who strive for a brighter future back home.

AYAN HASSAN studied at Wellstone International High School in Minneapolis.

DAHABO MOHAMED is a freshman in high school. She loves shopping, traveling, and learning new languages. So far she has been to more than twenty countries and can fluently speak six languages (English, Somali, Arabic, Swahili, Dutch, and Swedish). She lives in Minneapolis, Minnesota, with her mom (whom she loves very much)!

FAIZO ABDI MOHAMED is a student at Rochester STEM Academy and lives in Rochester.

DR. FARTUN MOHAMED RN, DNP, lives in Minnesota with her husband and four children. She is a recent graduate from the University of Minnesota, Doctorate of Nursing Practice, Midwifery program. She received her Bachelor of Science in nursing from Minnesota State University–Mankato. She is passionate about caring for women and families and plans to work in the Twin Cities as a midwife. In her spare time, she enjoys traveling and being outdoors.

FIRDOWSA HASHIM is a high school student living in Minnesota. She spends her days going to school, reading books, and watching shows. Her favorite subjects are English and History. She hopes to one day travel the world.

HIBAQ MOHAMED is an educator, mother, and Somali-Minnesotan who is constantly driven by her love for literature in all its forms. As an immigrant and teacher, she understands the power that comes with securing one's own narrative and amplifying the voices of the unheard. She believes in the powerful role literacy can play in empowering those voices and inspiring generations to come.

IFRAH MANSOUR is a Somali refugee, Muslim, multimedia artist, and educator based in Minnesota. Her artwork explores trauma through the eyes of children to uncover the resiliencies of Blacks, Muslims, and refugees. She interweaves poetry, puppetry, films, and installations. She's been featured on the BBC and in *Vice*, *OkayAfrica*, *Star Tribune*, and *City Pages*. Her critically acclaimed production *How to Have Fun in a Civil War* premiered at the Guthrie Theatre and toured to greater cities in Minnesota. Her first national museum exhibition, "Can I touch it," premiered at the Minneapolis Institute of Arts. Her visual poem "I am a Refugee" is part of PBS's short film festival. "My Aqal, banned and blessed" premiered at the Queens Museum in New York.

ILHAAN ABDIKARIM was born in Minneapolis, Minnesota. Her main hobbies are art, writing, and reading. When she's bored out of her mind, she writes stories—she has written so many that she has lost count. Her dream is to travel outside the US and maybe even study abroad. She's also interested in graphic design and filming. One thing she'd like to do is publish her first book.

JABRIL HASSAN is a student at Ubah Medical Academy and lives in Minneapolis.

KHADIJA MOHAMED is a Somali girl from Minneapolis. She really enjoys reading and having fun with her family in her free time. Learning more about her culture and heritage is very important to her. She is a very curious and outgoing student who wants the best for herself, her peers, and everyone around her.

LEYLA SULEIMAN is a young professional about to embark on a teaching career. She completed the University of Minnesota's Master of Education and Teaching License Program this year, and plans to be a high school English language arts teacher. Leyla is passionate about transforming schools into liberating, joyful spaces for all youth. In addition to her work as an educator, she leads a youth group for high school Muslim girls in Woodbury, Minnesota, and enjoys traveling, writing, watching horror movies and romantic comedies, and studying the art of gourmet cooking.

MOHAMED ALI attends school in Rochester, Minnesota. Mohamed is a sophomore in high school, but plans to become a businessman for his career. He enjoys playing sports and video games in his free time. Mixed with two different nationalities, he speaks Somali, Arabic, and English.

MOHAMEDAMIN HUSSEIN enjoys learning new things. No matter what challenges he faces, he always comes out with a smile on his face.

MOHAMED HASSAN is a student at Step Academy and lives in St. Paul.

NASRA ABDIMALIK lives in Minneapolis, Minnesota. She is an enthusiastic person who loves to learn new languages, cultures, and people. When she isn't at school, she likes to go outside, write short stories, and help out in her community.

NAWAL ABDI is a sophomore at Southwest High School. She has always enjoyed reading and writing ever since she was little. Her favorite genres include fiction, nonfiction, and mystery. She is always active and enjoys the outdoors while spending time with the people around her.

QALI ABDI is a high school senior. She has loved writing her whole life. When she isn't indulging in a new YA book, you can find her enjoying international films. She lives in Minnesota with her family.

RODA ABDI is a writer who currently resides in Minnesota. She is a 2017 graduate of St. Catherine University, where she earned her Bachelor of Arts in English. This is the first time her writing has been published in an anthology, and she is excited about how an anthology of this nature will incite meaningful cultural conversation.

SAFI MOHAMED is a sophomore in high school. She's a very outgoing and friendly person, and she gets along with everyone. She is very adventurous and after high school she wants to travel the world and learn about other cultures, religions, and traditions. She's very inspired and when she has her eye on something, she can achieve it. She loves writing poems so she can tell her story. She lives in Brooklyn Park, Minnesota.

SARA OSMAN is a graduate from the Harvard Graduate School of Education and is transitioning into her first year of law school. Sara is from Minneapolis, Minnesota, and is a product of the city's thriving Somali community. She is currently working as the Director of Curriculum Development and Leadership for the Qalanjo Project, a Somali arts community organization in Minneapolis that she cofounded with her friends. Sara is a youth worker, organizer, writer, filmmaker, and above all, a storyteller who is passionate about uplifting the stories of her community.

SHADIA ESSA lives in Minneapolis, Minnesota. Soft-spoken and with a passion to write about the untold stories from her motherland, she's been given the gift of writing and making you feel like you're actually experiencing what she's telling. She's loud, outgoing, and has had the same best friends since she could remember: paper and pencil.

UGBAD BARUD graduated from Wellstone International High School in Minneapolis and currently attends Normandale Community College, where she is studying to be a midwife.

WASIMA FARAH is a digital artist based in Saint Paul, Minnesota. Her work centers women of color and varies from vibrant illustrations to graphic designs and videography. She is inspired by women's empowerment and uses primary colors to express a bold and confident message. Her goal is to create art that others can relate to, feel the message of, and be motivated from.

ZAMZAM AHMED studied at Wellstone International High School in Minneapolis.

Acknowledgments

Gratitude is due to every young writer who has courageously contributed their stories and poetry, some seen in this volume and others whose work remains valuable and connected to the project. The courage and authenticity of their words are the carriers of dreams, resilience, belief, and hope.

I would be remiss not to acknowledge the deep roots of this project in the Minnesota Humanities Center's (MHC) 2006–2008 Somali Bilingual Book Project. My deepest gratitude and appreciation to MHC for its enduring mission to create space for absent narratives; the publication of this anthology is a testimony to that mission. Sincere thanks to Kirk MacKinnon Morrow for his hard work and unflagging devotion to this project; to Eden Bart for rolling up her sleeves for hard work as it came; and to Casey DeMarais, Laura Benson, and David O'Fallon of MHC—it is because of your belief and valuable partnership that this anthology exists. To Dara Beevas and Alyssa Bluhm at Wise Ink for their invaluable guidance and for working tirelessly with us through both setbacks and successes to help us realize the publication of this anthology.

Special thanks to Joel Coleman, Daniel Aamot, Mia Waldera, and Tara Kennedy, and all the teachers for being cultural brokers for their students to tell their stories. Sincere appreciation to the members of the advisory group who helped shape the beginnings of the work that would become this anthology. Thank you as well to those who helped with suggestions, reviewed and edited, and offered input including the Somali-language portions of this text.

Thanks to Lisa Bullard for her astute advice; to Ebyan Abdiger for her journalistic eye to detail; Safiyo Dhuux for being a bookworm; to Abdiwahab Dahir and Ahmed Yusuf for Afka-hooyo (mother-tongue) and Walaaltinimo (brotherhood) ama Soomaalinimo; to Bruce Drewlow for seeking to promote human welfare through education and relatedness; to Professors Martha Bigelow and Abdi Warfa for their friendship and the vision to broaden the landscape of our reach as educators; to Professor Pauline Boss, whose book Ambiguous Loss broke the spell for me with the right language to finally begin processing the complexities of the "ambiguous losses in the lives of individuals and families living through the ambiguities of war and displacement."

The dedication of this anthology is offered in two parts: to children and youth around the world whose lives were impacted by movements and journeys, and the negotiations one must make in those spaces of marginality; and to my village of family and friends.

—Marian A. Hassan

Waari mayside war ha kaa haro.

YOU WON'T LIVE FOREVER;
LEAVE A LEGACY.